GIFT OF THE DREAMTIME

Awakening to the Divinity of Trauma

By

S. Kelley Harrell

Foreword by Christina Pratt, author of

An Encyclopedia of Shamanism

Soul Intent Arts
Fuquay Varina, North Carolina USA

PRAISE FOR GIFT OF THE DREAMTIME

Harrell draws you into the dreamtime as an expert novelist draws you into a great novel and shares with you her experiences and knowledge of the world beyond the veil from the time she was very young. ~ *Innerchange Magazine*

In this book that hunger and fear that nibbled and clawed at you and me for years is explained in poetic, experiential detail. Kelley guides us into our own souls, turning the "whys" into wise. ~ Bridgett Walther, author of *Conquer the Cosmos*

Let S. Kelley Harrell guide you on a very special spiritual journey — destination your healed soul! ~ Donna Henes, author of *The Queen of My Self*

Absolutely recommend *Gift of the Dreamtime* to anyone, especially those working to overcome their own traumas. *~Facing North*

Kelley Harrell acts as a guide to help us move from deep trauma to wisdom. A brave book, beautifully insightful, that leads us to greater knowing of ourselves. ~ Gail Wood, author of *The Shamanic Witch*

Gift of the Dreamtime gives hope for those of us who sometimes feel we're not doing things right, or that perhaps there is no healing to be had. *~Pagan Book Reviews*

Gift of the Dreamtime – Awakening to the Divinity of Trauma
By S. Kelley Harrell
© 2012, Second Edition

Foreward by Christina Pratt
Edited by Peggy Payne
Cover Art: Cathy McKinty
Cover Design: S. Kelley Harrell

Published by: Soul Intent Arts, LLC,
Fuquay Varina, NC 27526
dreamtime@soulintentarts.com
www.soulintentarts.com

First Edition published in 2004 by Spilled Candy Enterprises

ISBN: 978-0986016516 (trade paperback)
First printing: July 2012
Printed in the United States of America
A Soul Intent Arts Publication

This book is available in print and as an ebook. Visit kelleyharrell.com for information on Kelley's other books and publications.

ALSO BY KELLEY

Gift of the Dreamtime Reader's Companion

Real Wyrd – A Modern Shaman's Roots in the Middle World

DEDICATION

to rob
maya and tristan
mom, lloyd, and ellen
jacob and elizabeth
my spirit teachers, here
and There
—my love and thanks for you.

ACKNOWLEDGEMENTS

Greatest thanks to Lorna Tedder for originally lighting the page with the words that burned in my head; to Christina Pratt for her eagerness to leap forward with compassion, over and over.

Thanks to Cathy McKinty for the use of her beautiful artwork; to Peggy Payne for impeccable wordsmithing; to my trusty peer readers for bearing the news; to Ai Gvhdi Waya, Kristin Madden, and Peter Aziz—thank you for your honesty and willingness to answer my questions when I first began this spirited word journey.

FOREWORD

I have participated in and contributed to the growth of neoshamanism in North America over the past decades as the founding director of *Last Mask Center for Shamanic Healing* and the author of the two-volume set, *An Encyclopedia of Shamanism*. I am part of a small, slowly growing group of authentic, non-traditional shamans who have had to establish ourselves alone and solely through the value of our work. Kelley Harrell stands as a strong presence in this small, yet powerful circle of heart-centered shamanism. I have great respect for Kelley, who, like myself, does not claim academic degrees or indigenous pedigree to validate her work. She claims only the right and freedom to do her work as she is called to do so by Spirit.

People come to my center in Portland, Oregon, proud and burdened by gifts they've had since childhood, like seeing the spirits of the dead or having "the touch" that takes away the pain of others. Very few will lay down their individuality and personality to "be cooked by Spirit" in the training necessary to accurately and effectively use their gifts. Clients share their "shamanic healing crises" with me weekly as if it is completed, without realizing that they are still in it and will likely remain so until death. They don't realize how few will actually muster the determination, crazy logic, and disciplined chaos necessary to walk away from everything they know and hold dear and find their own path out of the maze of their own disease and suffering.

Kelley has done both and we get to see it unfold, page after page. With the gift of her excellent prose she is able take the reader by the heart and retrace the steps she takes on her journey with Spirit. For those of you interested in shamanism you can experience a shaman finding her shaman legs, reshaping the workings of her mind, and awakening her courageous heart. For the rest of you this is a story of healing. It is an inspiration for those who have suffered great trauma, like incest, chronic violence, or the soul loss induced by the daily, normal horrors of war, and refuse to be hobbled or accept anything less than the life you came here to live.

Students of shamanism continuously ask how to journey better. *Gift of the Dreamtime* is a great guide for how to journey, without ever explaining how to do anything. There is a knack to working with Spirit that is part instinct, part perseverance, part intuition, and part hitch up your britches and hang on. It's nearly impossible to teach to those who have no instinct for it. In these pages the student of shamanism can watch that mastery being born. Kelley is such an excellent writer that you are right there in her journeys with her, knowing the questions, feeling the confusion or brilliance of the answers, and sensing the ring of truth. The reader can feel the power in the messages even when we, and Kelley, have no idea how to interpret them yet or what they will mean. I truly enjoyed this authenticity and find it unique in writing about shamanism. In working with spirit shamanically, we do not always get comfort when we think we want it, answers are often completely unclear even when they ring true, and often we do not like the answer because it hurts and will be hard to do. This struggle and the patience, trust, and intuition necessary to unfold it into the clarity of a path are beautifully rendered here. If you want to understand what journeying with spirit means; read, watch, and learn.

I liked this book, when I honestly cannot get through most others of this genre because they have no guts. Kelley is not afraid to feel and to show us those feelings before she tidies up. Feelings are messy things.

They show up where we don't want them to be and they don't show up where we feel they should be. They hide, we seek, and when they do appear they are nothing like we expected. And if we don't accept all of this we cannot truly heal. Feelings are like water, they flow following their own logic. We must learn to develop our own felt sense of our inner reality if we are to gain the wisdom of the emotional body. Again and again Kelley's path turns on her ability to unlock the wisdom of her true emotions. By example, Kelley shows us how to do what most books can only tell us to do. *"… sit with a feeling, acknowledge it. Don't try to change it or find a source for it. Don't analyze it. Just sit with it."* And by doing so we are rewarded as the amazing web of connection and interconnection of this healing story emerges, making each of the associations and revelations unique and necessary apparent for her true freedom from emotional suffering.

The most important quality of Kelley's storytelling is how she shows us that the path to self love is arduous and not for the faint of heart. Every healer will tell you that you must love yourself and they all make it sound like it's pat and easy, just affirm it 300 times a day with your crystal, tap here, detox there and you are all set. However love, true love, is a perfectly, hard path. I am not talking here about the small loves of everyday life, but of, as Kelley says, *"…perfect love, not a lover or a parent, not a teacher or guide. It's all of those and more, at once… It's not sexual, not romantic, not parental, not platonic, but somehow all of those. (It's) all the love I've felt for anything and everything in all my life, all at once."* This is the true love that heals all things. I was inspired by Kelley's fierce commitment to living in a way that loves everything and everyone, without exception, and taking the path to get there. Her story exposes the understanding that it is the true nature of our soul's human existence to love, only to love.

In an overwhelming field of self-help and pop shamanism Kelley Harrell offers a book that actually does help, gives us a rare view into authentic shamanism, and can be used as a champion for your own real healing. This is a work of non-fiction that takes place entirely in the Dreamtime of shamanic journeys and nighttime sleeping dreams. This is a true story: the loss and trepidation of surrender is not airbrushed out, the confusion and angry frustration of working with Spirit is right there with the joys and inspiration, the blood, sweat, time, and tears of deep healing are all right here. This is the true story, the whole passionate and messy story of a woman's healing from incest in which each step was necessary, but no step was "good enough." Like all true stories, this story does not end until the healer/warrior arrives home in the profoundly ordinary peace and divinity of her own heart.

Christina L Pratt

Director, *Last Mask Center for Shamanic Healing*

Author, *An Encyclopedia of Shamanism*

Portland, Oregon

2012

Path of the Dreamtime

When *Gift of the Dreamtime* was first published in 2004, there was no accessible framework in western literature for the modern shamanic narrative. Our perception of that story lay between ancient and indigenous echoes, and biased academic assertions. In the west, we learned of shamanism in the rearview, from the witnessing of those who have benefitted from it without sharing the inner process for how they got there. The missing narrative is the collection of symbols we each carry, telling the story of our bodies, minds and souls. Shamans peer into these narratives to decode them, to extract from them the deepest core of our wellbeing and enliven us with our own power, once again.

Many stories exist of western seekers venturing into other cultures for help from tribal spiritual leaders, and they are wonderful. I wanted to offer something different. Through sharing my story I wanted to give a glimpse into the process of moving from post-traumatic stress through the dynamic of the wounded healer, to someone who thrives beyond the wound in *this* culture, using the spiritual resources of *this* place. Such an act of present manifestation is the modern shamanic narrative. This is the power we all carry.

The publishing of this book and its warm reception around the world brought me in touch with many new people on similar journeys, a gift for which I remain grateful. In that time *Soul Intent Arts* has become a thriving local and international shamanic practice. Through it I've been able to travel and meet many of my readers in-person, teaching them the soul way to decode their own stories for healing and empowerment.

As I began to receive mail from readers, I realized that there was indeed not just an audience deeply interested in connecting with the stories of others on extraordinary spiritual journeys, but a tribe deeply devoted to creating wellbeing for themselves and for All Things. In an effort to more thoroughly address questions about the path of the modern shaman, in 2004 I created my blog, *Intentional Insights – Q&A From Within*. Since then, this open dialogue with souls has gained a lively worldwide audience through addressing reader inquiries regarding implementing shamanistic approaches into modern living and co-creating with the unseen in everyday life.

Furthering that outreach, in 2010 I created *The Tribe of the Modern Mystic* as both a community helping intuitives assimilate spiritual emergency, and an online distance mystery school to create space for those ready to broaden their awareness with intention.

My personal path has been animistic since 1988, and since 2000 I have worked with others as a shaman. Culturally speaking, ours is a broken path. We cannot claim what is not ours, and we cannot deny inherent truths that are. Thank you for helping me to realize some of my truths. Thank you for witnessing my path. Thank you for helping this book continue its journey.

For more information about me, my other publications, newsletter, *Intentional Insights*, *Soul Intent Arts*, or *The Tribe of the Modern Mystic*, visit www.soulintentarts.com. A Reader's Companion to *Gift of the Dreamtime* can also be found at kelleyharrell.com.

Dream well,

~skh

2012

Into all of life's dark places
obscured with the objects
of our time,
from the ancestors' hands
and beyond their star bodies,
let the light shine
and the shaman see;
let the transformation begin.

PROLOGUE

He's making pizza when we arrive.

I climb up on a chair next to the counter so that I stand level with the frozen pie covered with strips of ham and plastic cheese. He asks me if I like adding things to pizzas, and I say yes. Mama kisses me and leaves for the church meeting as I pile on sandwich meat.

He smiles at me as he gives me more ham to arrange, asks what I want to do for the evening. I say I don't know, and he slides our supper into the oven as we focus on the news, and I think this time, maybe this time will be different.

But as we sit down to eat, I feel his hand on my knee and I try to keep my eyes above the table because I know if I look down, it will be out and I don't want to see it. My pizza tastes like nothing and I think I looked, but I didn't mean to.

The couch is always crowded with him, and I have to lie that much closer and I'm cold where my skin is exposed. His hands are there. He asks me if I like it, but I say no and he sounds surprised. I reconsider and decide I don't like it, though I reconsider.

He tells me to touch where he's out and I do, but I must have done it wrong because he tells me I don't have to. So I don't anymore, and I look down from somewhere above us.

He says we are playing, but I just feel burning, there, like when I'm sick, like when I have to go to the doctor, and I wonder if I will have to go to the doctor again because I'm burning. He asks me if it feels good and I say no. He asks me if I like to play and I say no, but I don't think he believes me because he keeps playing.

He tells me that I am special and that we have a secret, and that I can spend the night, and that if I spend the night, we can play all night and no one will know. And I suddenly see us in his room and I feel really warm in his bed, like I'm special, but I don't want to be in his room so I stop seeing it. I say I don't want to spend the night, and he says I don't have to.

I know the TV is on but all I see is its blue haze over the room, the mirror on the mantle. I watch the reflection, hoping to see something there that will stop this, looking for Mama's headlights for when she will be back to get me. I think of how a seven-year-old would never put up with this, how tomorrow is my birthday, and everything will be different then, and how after I'm a year older, I won't let this happen anymore. I see myself in my Wonder Woman Underoos, a super power saving the world, saving them all, and then I see her headlights in the mirror lighting the room. He must have seen them, too, because we stop playing and he jumps up and I know things will be different tomorrow. Starting tomorrow, I'll make them different.

 ONE

The group is nervous as the ritual begins. The energy of the room rises with the calling in of the directions. We watch the shaman turn to face each direction, rattling and whistling, inviting each one as she calls for the souls of each of us to create the sacred space to do her work. It's an odd situation as we are all strangers coming together to learn a very personal thing. The room is small, crowded still by our bodies strewn over blankets on the floor, our notepads waiting by our fingertips, scarves to blot out the tiniest hints of light.

But we don't need to see. The shaman is going to teach us to see with our other eyes, how to let our souls journey out of our bodies to find our power animals and guides. She says we all have them, spirit guides who watch over us, and that she will teach us how to communicate with them in trance. According to the shaman, we will meet these special beings in the spirit worlds of the Dreamtime.

I think I know what will be there when I arrive. I've felt it waiting for me for the last twenty-six years, but I don't know how to get there on my own. The shaman knows, she and her drum. The steady rhythm she beats from it carries me to the places that I need to go.

From the first drum beat, everything I see is vivid, clear. This is the Middle World, the dwelling place of the soul of the Earth. From this middle place, I will reach the other spirit realms. All I did was close my eyes and listen to the drum to get here. There was no struggle to leave my body, no fear, just opening up from the inside. I don't recognize where I am exactly, but that's OK. It *feels* right. The tangy aroma of damp earth and pine forest greet me. A small pond with a waterfall spilling into it captures my attention. It's the only thing here that's moving and alive.

I dip my fingers into the water and it slips cool around my hand, tugging me in. The grip says something is behind the waterfall, waiting for me, and the only way to find out what is to dive in.

The air is warm and balmy, but the water cools me. Deep down, the spilling fall breaks into calm, and I dive beneath it, rising up behind the liquid curtain to rock steps leading through an opening.

This is what I was looking for! I'm seeing the portal to my Lower World for the first time! Peering up the rock steps and into the narrow stone passage, I amble up the slight grade toward the pale blue sky at the end. Water trickles down my back and my hair drips into my face as I follow the horizontal striations of white in the mocha-colored rock wall, smudgy lines pointing to my Lower World. Pushing my hair from my eyes, I shake off the tingle pricking my cool skin, excitement pounding in my chest. What will I meet here—animal guides who watch over me? What if I don't have guides? What if there's nothing for me at all?

Maybe the portal itself is the treasure, that I could even get this far outside myself. I like it here. Safe stone comfort, mist rising from the fall behind me, its splashes echoing in the tiny corridor. I like the Dreamtime. I could stay here forever and never go back. Nothing in my waking world is this peaceful.

Something's brushing against me. Wings! What feels like huge wings flutter behind me, head to toe, feathers tickling, urging me forward. The shaman said not to look for animals on this first journey. She said not to do anything but find the portal and follow it through to my Lower World, the place where I can heal. Something or someone else is already here, though, behind me, and I can't stop it from pushing me further into the cave.

Inching slowly along before this unseen host, an odd rock juts out into the path of the portal, almost completely blocking the way. It's a tight squeeze around it. The damp rock wall leaves a wet smudge on my shirt and a chill across my belly. Through the tiny opening at the other end, the blue sky gets closer, bigger with every step, breaking into the full landscape of a sunlit valley.

Standing in the opening, I hold my breath, looking out over my Lower World. I couldn't have created a more perfect setting. Birds sing in the trees, though I don't feel feathers behind me anymore. A breeze blows, swirling in the arch of the portal and blowing my hair back into my face. Straight ahead of me, the ground slopes to a clearing cut by a stream. A mountain rises just beyond the swiftly moving water.

To the left is a hill rising beyond a thick dark forest, an odd tree perched at its crest. The tree stands out, clearly not part of the forest, though it doesn't look any different from the other trees. Yet it *is* different. I can tell it is just by observing it from within the safety of my portal. The hill where the tree sits is a perfect vantage point, its rolling edge jutting out over the valley. That would be a great thinking spot, in spite of the strange tree. I'm sure I could see everything from that overlook.

That hill swells into ripples of hills beyond, breaching ridges and a chain of foothills, then hazy mountains as far as I can see. At the center of the slope, straight down from my portal, is the stream rushing into a small pond with an even smaller pier. The pond trickles to a lazy creek off to the right, seemingly into nowhere. It doesn't end, I just can't see where the creek goes from there. In fact, as I take in the perimeter, the entire landscape fades to a blur at the edges. After a certain point, the water is the sky, the trees are the land, the mountains are the clouds. There are no defined qualities beyond the immediate valley where I stand.

Apart from that weird tree, there is one other thing that distinguishes itself in the valley. A sand circle sits on the bank above the disappearing creek, sparse trees beyond. I don't know what the circle is for. The circle has been very carefully placed well away from the stream and the forest, and it is perfectly round. The faint lines traced in the sand divide it into sections, its blunt border reminding me loosely of a baseball diamond. I really hope it doesn't have anything to do with baseball.

The most remarkable thing that I see, normal as it seems, is the pier. That concerns me. The tree is odd, but it's still just a tree. Even the sand circle, so carefully placed in lush green grass, seems to be appropriate in some primal way. The pier is the only thing not of nature in this pristine setting. I walk down the slope to examine it closer, without getting too close. If I built it, I don't remember doing it. And if I didn't, who did?

I've no sooner formed the thought than the ground begins to tremble and there's a great pounding, rumbling to a horrific roar as a herd of mustangs charges at me from across the sand circle. I could make it back to the portal before they reach me, if I could move. But I don't. I can't. I'm frozen in place, not even breathing as the ground shakes. I close my eyes, bracing to be trampled.

The shaman said this might happen, that sometimes in journey, the animals dismember you to heal you. They take you apart, then put you back together without affliction. She didn't say it would be this real. The pounding of their hooves is all around me, and I can't tell it from my heart or the shaman's beating drum. I just keep my eyes closed tight as the ground quakes to the point that I don't think I can stand, and I don't know how I'm not falling. It seems like they should have passed me by now, but they keep rushing by. The clods of earth slung from their hooves sting my legs.

Somehow I'm still standing, though, and as I open my eyes, I see that I'm the center of their mad dash as they've formed two uniform lines racing pell mell on either side of me. They are intentionally running around me, otherwise, not acknowledging me at all.

Who are they, and what do they mean? Everything here means something, and I know I should ask, but *how*?

Standing among them, I feel the power of their race until they've gone, completely disappeared into the forest at the base of the hill with the strange tree.

Panting, I look around, bracing for what may come next. I have just enough time to collect myself and realize that I really *did* get here when I hear the shaman's drumbeat shift from steady low pounding to the quick loud staccato of the callback, telling me it's time to return to my body.

Somewhere in the fury I started crying, though I don't know exactly when or why. It's not from fear. It's from...*excitement*?

I walk up the slope to the portal, trembling down the stone passage and through the fall. I don't open my eyes yet, but I know I'm back in the room with our group. As I sit up and wipe the tears from my cheeks, my heart is still pounding, my hands shaking. But when it's my turn to describe my first shamanic journey to everyone, I have no words to describe the beauty and power of my Lower World.

When everyone has spoken about their first journeys, we prepare for the next one: meet the Lower World. I think I met mine already, up close and personal, but I listen closely to the instructions. This time as the shaman's drum pounds, I'm planning to step out into my Lower World and try not to get stampeded.

Taking a deep breath, I relax into the dive beneath the fall, squeezing past the jutting rock in the passage of my portal. I'm halfway to the light beyond my portal before I realize there are no feathers pushing me along this time. Just the same, something is watching me walk down the grassy green hillside, down to the pond. Don't know what. Can't see what. Just feel it, know it's there.

From the small pier, I watch the gentle swirls of water foam and drift to the pond, where they relax into demure ripples. A short walk beyond the pond, up the mountain, and I peer down into a village, inhabited, but there are no people, no animals. An ocean lies beyond the village, its mist wrapping the huts and tents by the bare earth paths at the mountain's base.

From up here, I'm looking down on the hill crest and its strange solitary inhabitant. Even from a distance I can tell that tree is hollow, though it's very much alive and healthy. I sense that its roots have no end, that I could stand upright in its trunk and follow the root system to other places, other worlds, climb its branches far above the clouds. That's not such a strange idea. The shaman said the worlds of the Dreamtime are connected, and this tree is somehow that part of that connection.

I'm at the highest peak that I can see in the range of mountains looking out over the landscape of my Lower World...and I feel it looking back at me. I wonder if Columbus noticed the land of the New World staring back at him when he first saw it and if he had any idea what it had in store for him as he paced off its breadth and made his own plans. I know I didn't discover this place. But it will be where I discover myself.

I don't feel the need to explore the land any further. From up here, I see everything I need to. I sit, looking out over everything until the shaman's drum echoes the beginning rhythm of callback through my valley. Running full tilt down the mountain, through the stream, and up the slope, I feel the grasses of the Dreamtime tickle my ankles as I skip and twirl, arms above my head.

So much better than dancing with the lights off in my living room, I'm in the sun here, running free. And again, I'm crying as I run back, and whatever I sense hiding here, watching my silly dance, I don't care.

We are to meet an animal this time. Perhaps I'll find more than the feel of feathers, a frenzied stampede, and a world looking back at me. I'm supposed to meet my animal guide and learn what it brings to my life.

The smooth rock no longer juts out halfway through my portal but is flush with the lined cave wall. I don't know why it's moved or how, only that once I step in from the rocky steps behind the fall, I can see clear all the way through to the sky on the other side, and I can walk the whole length of it without brushing against a single dripping rock.

From the opening on the other side, I see a form on the pier—an owl, perched perfectly still. As I get closer, I see mottled browns, grays, and whites cover his wings and chest. A dark circle frames a face of tannish-beige, pointing downward between his eyes. When I step onto the pier, his smooth mask blinks at me but is otherwise solemnly still, no discernible expression at all. He's big for his kind, a barred owl, I think. He stands almost four feet tall next to me.

He looks peacefully out over the water, and his silence is so reverent that I hate to break it. But my curiosity is killing me.

"Who are you?" I ask, trembling. I'm pretty sure he's my animal guide, but I'd like to have his word.

"I am Allusius." He turns to me when he speaks. I hear his voice as plainly as I hear any person's. It's not internal or magickally perceived. He *speaks*, and his voice is raspy, like an old man's.

"Are you my animal guide?" My heart's pounding so hard I can barely get the words out. I just want to be sure.

"Yes."

Completely unintentionally, I let out a huge sigh, marveling at this creature studying me. Owls in books, owls in zoos, Pooh's owl, hooting in the night...that's all I know of them. It's in the Dreamtime that I truly see my first, and I feel somewhat like a bad hostess who doesn't know the tastes of her guests.

I consider various means of getting-to-know, courtesies to segué into the things I really want to know. Just as I'm getting ready to open up witty conversation, the owl launches himself straight at me, feet first, and decks me squarely between the eyes. The force of him knocks me flat on my back, and I'm breathless and stunned.

When I open my eyes, I'm soaring against a dark blue sky, high above treetops. I'm an owl. My hair isn't flying back in the breeze, no clothes whipping in the wind. I have feathers and precise control over my body. I'm impervious to the cold, fearless of heights. I see for miles, even through the shadowed forest. A glow emanates from everything I see, like tiny campfires obscured by height and trees. I hear the smallest movements in the stillest brush. I am my senses and nothing more, and I know this is what Allusius brings me. I know that I have shapeshifted into him, and that's how I can experience this flight. I also know in this experience of being him, that for his quiet demeanor and undisturbed visage, there's nothing subtle about him.

I land in my body back at the pier, and he resumes his stance, back toward me, staring at the water as if he didn't just knock me out and we didn't just fly above my Lower World. I honor his silence, but mostly I try to catch my breath.

Settling back on the pier beside him, I tuck my legs beneath me and ask, "How do I move beyond all the things going on in my life right now?"

He's gone. Was here, but now he's not. There's just me, the pier, the water, and the fear that I just don't know the protocol of communicating in this place.

I look back up the slope and over to the sand circle, but he's nowhere to be seen. Maybe I did something wrong? In her instructions, the shaman said that guides can be tricky this way, forcing you to ask what you really mean. She said if that happens, call the animal back, try it *another way*.

"Allusius?" I call out.

Instantly he's perched on the pier, gazing into the pond, and I'm relieved.

"How do I live this life and be myself?" That's a little more specific.

"Just *live* it!" he bellows. I think I've angered him, but when I look into his face, I see myself reflected, like I'm sort of in a daze somewhere outside of myself, observing. I see me putting one foot in front of the other like some automaton, watching a butterfly as I eat my lunch in the park, feeling the cold wood of the floor beneath my feet as I head down the hall to bed, cursing the screech of the alarm clock as it signifies this pattern will completely repeat tomorrow. I watch myself go through this routine, missing so many details of my life, particularly the winged shadow that follows above me every step I take. I look lonely going through this routine, but I'm never alone and I've met the reason why: I've met Allusius, my primary animal totem.

Just live it, indeed. We sit looking into the water, my toes just barely grazing its surface, until the drum once again pulls me back to waking. This time I'm not crying as I sit up. When it's my turn to discuss the meeting with my animal guide, I consider how to explain this experience but say only, "I met an owl. He doesn't talk much."

For this journey, we're to take it a bit further with the animal, ask it a question, get its insight into an aspect of our lives.

I don't tell the shaman that I've already taken it further with Allusius, but I think it's okay. It feels okay with him.

Still, I do it the way she tells us this time, by forming an intention. I ask my guide to help me find the soul parts of me that I know are still missing, then dive beneath the fall.

An auburn horse is just outside the portal. I sense that she's a mother, young, but weathered the birth of a foal and its selling.

"Are you an animal guide?" I ask. Allusius isn't here, and she doesn't reply.

Ride, I hear. From that I know, she is a helper, only here for this brief visit. She's not a guide who will stay by my side for this life. It appears once again that I'm slightly off-track in following instructions for this journey.

I mount her, bareback, petting her sides and mane as we walk. Over the crest of the mountain, down into the blue mist of the village, her gait is slow and easy, our motion fluid. We glide so easily, it's hard to believe that we've never taken this ride together before.

"You're a helper, right? A teacher?" I'm anxious, and her silence tells me that I'm pushing and need to relax. I want to know what each detail of this place brings my life, what it means, how I can learn from it. I want to know it all!

She walks on as if I haven't spoken, quietly strolling down the dirt path of the settlement, the heavy mist not obscuring her careful steps.

"How do I find the pieces of me that I haven't been able to bring back?"

The whole purpose of this journey is to get information from my guide about something in my life, and I'm getting nothing. She's not even my guide. I must be doing something wrong.

Still, her silence quiets me. I think she can talk; she just isn't for some reason, which means I must listen closer. I comb through the meaning of her silence, pondering everything I've experienced here so far as my fingers fan through her mane.

She walks until we reach the shoreline beyond the dwellings. Foamy waves lap gently on the shore, and looking out across the water, I see that occasionally the mist parts to reveal split seconds of calm seas. We stand watching the haze ride the water until she turns, goes a few more steps down the beach, then stops again, facing out over the sea. Over and over, walking, stopping, turning, until we have walked the length of the shore, peering out over the water.

I don't understand what it is that she wants me to see, what she's trying to tell me. Frustrated, I quiet my racing mind, listening to the lulling surf, feeling the spray gently tickle my toes, my body shifting slightly with her subtle movements.

After a few moments, the mist dissipates, and I see it. Not too far across the sea is a heavily forested island. The same mist hovers there, dark, though glints of silver occasionally catch, reflecting the dew hugging the heavy blue leaves of the treetops.

We stand there for what seems like hours, the sun moving to set, looking toward the mysterious isle. Then I realize why she's not talking, why she brought me here. Looking across the water to this shrouded island, I understand that it's not hidden at all. I just couldn't see it before. Resting my head against hers, we stare at that island, and I know that nothing about me has ever been lost. I just need to know how to see it.

Up, up. It's a different portal, to get to my Upper World, and already, it's so different from the one to my Lower World. From the top level of the dimly starlit room in my crown chakra, I step through its door, out into the damp haze of the clouds in my Upper World.

There are no animals here, only spirit guides, guardians, angels, clouds, and blue. The shaman said that someone has chosen to watch over me lifelong, someone I'm here to find, just as I found Allusius in the Lower World.

I climb the clouds, heaped atop each other. When I top the fourth mound I know I have arrived. Where, exactly, I don't know, but here I am. I'm alone, with nothing but clouds layered with blue sky as far as the eye.

There's a man! An older man in silvery white robes approaches from my left. His robes float around him more than he wears them. If I could touch them, they would be gossamer, cool mist raising bumps on my skin, like riding bareback through the mist of the hazy village.

But I dare not touch. I just know and watch him walk toward me.

I know him. I have awakened to him standing at the foot of my bed in the dead of night. I saw him once before as I crept down the hall of my Mom's house in the wee hours, the back of my neck stirring with the footsteps behind me, his silver hem catching the corner of my eye when I turned to look back. I never knew who he was, but each time I dove under the covers and didn't come out until the sun rose.

He looks like Merlin without the hat but every bit as majestic. His name is Simon, and he tells me he's my spirit guide without me even having to ask. It's a pretty big switch from getting stampeded and knocked between the eyes. I expect other aspects of this Upper World are even different still.

"Are you my only spirit guide? Are there others?"

"Yes, many. But I am the only constant." He speaks as he paints swirling lines of primary colors onto a white canvas propped on an easel, all of which a moment before were not here. Lines, dipping, crossing, colors contrasting, distinguished, but they never mask each other out even when they overlap. Their colors never blend, and I can't tell if that's something that Simon controls or if that's just the way paint behaves here. My guess is the former, though I didn't come to discuss the physics of art.

"How can I get out of the slump of depression?" I ask him, for this is the intention I've chosen for our meeting.

"You already are. You have worked hard."

I squint at him, considering that life can be free of depression, not just consumed by the persistent management of it. I've never thought of that before.

"Yes, but what do I do?" There must be something—a ritual, something I have to do or change, give up.

"Oh, you will do a great thing here that will reach the lives of many."

That's not what I meant, but I'll go with it. "You mean, I'll write a book?" I blurt out. It's my first thought. I'm not sure where it comes from, though I can't imagine doing anything other than writing. It's... what I do.

Silence. His expression is perplexed, taut. I don't think this is going in the direction either of us wants it to. He rests his paintbrush on his palette, then paces, and I reframe.

"What do I need to do about the depression?"

He paces more, then says, "Let it go."

"How?"

"You will. You're already doing it."

"But what is the depression? Where did it come from? Don't I need to address its origin to let it go?" It can't be as simple as just letting go. I think I would have thought of that on my own if it were.

He stops pacing then and looks directly at me. I freeze in his pale blue eyes, afraid that I've already tried his patience and we've only just met. Very calmly, he says, "Look to the things to which it makes you sensitive."

I look, but my whole life comes to mind. Nothing stands out at all—just stress, sex, digestion, deadlines, bright light, traffic jams, a fantastic book, colors in sunsets, tears, the right person saying my name, giggles coming out of nowhere. It's not so easy as just bad or sad to make me feel so much at once that I want to hide for a while. I feel everything with the same intensity.

"But depression makes me sensitive to everything. Almost as if ..." I begin, then stop.

He nods, urging me to finish.

"Almost as if... if I didn't have depression, there would be feelings I would've never felt, good, bad, or otherwise. Things I never would have perceived at all because depression is what makes me sensitive that those feelings are even *there*?" I mean it to be a statement, but it comes out more like a question.

He stops nodding, presses his palms together, and gives me a steady gaze.

It seems sensible, rational...somehow. I nod, continuing to reason it out, things becoming clearer as I talk. "It's intuition, isn't it? Depression is intuition that I don't express, and if I just express those feelings, no matter how nuts they seem, there's no need for depression."

His smile is kind, along with his eyes, and he says only, "What do you *feel* that depression is?"

I know what it is now. And I know trying not to be sensitive and holding in my feelings and perceptions isn't the solution anymore. Moreover, it never was.

I don't know what this will mean in my life, really. But he's right. Seeing that depression is willful repression of myself, I *can* just let it go. There's nothing for me to do *except* let it go, because I feel what I feel. I know the things that I sense and see, things that others don't.

Callback begins. I thank him and run back, leaping through the portal, sliding down the banister of the stairs in my heart.

This is the last journey of the day, the one in which we seek healing. We don't have to tell each other what we find this time, just hold our intentions in mind, take them to the animal guide.

I know part of me is sick. It has been all of my life, and I need to find information for healing it. The infections — my bladder needs me, as everything else I've tried has failed. I intend to find what will work.

The slope of my Lower World is clear and free. No one waits at the other side of the portal this time, but Allusius is perched on the edge of the pier, facing the pond. That pier is his place. I know now that I can always find him there, and that assurance is priceless to me.

I don't know him well yet, but my chest is exploding with little flutters at seeing him. He just makes me feel so happy, and in his presence, my worries are small.

I'm smiling like a fool because from behind his one expression, he's happy to see me, too. He doesn't show it in the least, and somehow my joy is greater *feeling* his desire to visit with me.

"May I ask you about something?"

"What is it?" he replies.

"I'm sick."

He tilts his head then gives me a quizzical look. I'm taken aback to have elicited a different expression from him

"I have a bladder infection. I have them a lot, since I was little. What can I do about them?"

"Doctor."

I think carefully before I speak. "The doctors I've seen give me medicines that make other parts of me sick and don't fix what was already sick."

"Don't go to those doctors."

Funny owl tells me what I know, only I know it more now that he's said it.

"Hmm. Alternative doctor, maybe?"

"Yes," he affirms, flashing his expressionless visage. "What causes these infections to recur?"

"You have much energy there."

My abdomen churns under his words, and I'm perplexed. I've felt that low rumble before, but I never knew what it was. "What kind of energy?"

"Hatred." The word comes effortlessly from him, though I struggle to hear it.

Do I hate? I have hated. I don't hate anyone now, but I trust Allusius. Something is making me stay sick, and if he says it's there, I trust his judgment.

"Hatred?"

"Yes. It reminds you."

His stoic eyes stare back at the shock that I don't try to hide. I'm utterly speechless, though I'm not surprised by his implication. Because it's the truth doesn't make it any easier to hear.

I lie still while others rustle around me in their journeys. Silently I pray that they have no idea what is happening in mine. I don't like where this is going, although I walked myself right here. When I find my voice, I hear myself agreeing with Allusius.

"Yes. Yes, it does remind me." Admitting that, I feel alone and very small. I understand that doctors and medicines can't fix hate. They don't notice where bodies shouldn't have been touched or the things that get left behind in bodies when they're hurt, when they burn, or what burning makes brains think of. Years ago, I quit taking medicines and hating people because both were killing me. Until now, I never learned, never understood not to hate the burning.

I'd recompose myself if it were possible. But I'm here with my owl, getting what I came for. So why not just put it all on the table?

"How do I heal it?" I whisper.

"Give it love. Take *care* of this part of you." He says it matter-of-factly, like a doctor dictating a prescription.

I have no response. No words from me can qualify his truth further. I know what love is. It's what I feel for the things that make me happy, yet I can never explain the feeling, itself. It's what I give to the things that make me sad when nothing else has made them happy. I consider his suggestion, weighing if I can actually carry it out, and realize it is indeed now all on the table. I can't take it back. I have to learn to love this part of me, because the burning ultimately is *part* of me.

"Can I hug you?" I ask him, timidly. I've put things on tables before and been met with nothing in return. Allusius doesn't seem to be a huggish type, but no harm in asking. Moreover, I'm shaking so badly, I think I'm going fall over if someone doesn't hold me up.

He doesn't move but passively permits me to enfold him. After a few seconds, feathers give me a familiar light pat on the shoulder, and I know I'm not alone or falling over.

He knows, like no one in my waking world could. He knows why I've come to the Dreamtime and what I have that needs healing. In such a short time, he's taught me so much. I must keep in mind that when I ask questions here, I get answers — the right answers — whether it's what I want to hear, it's what I *need* to hear. And I've gotten the answer I came for this time.

I thank him, then run up the slope. I have one foot in the portal, but I don't want to leave. Something feels unfinished. Looking back at him, I see that he's still on the pier. Something about his perpetual staring at the water seems sad, an emptiness all its own. Concerned, I ask him if he's okay.

"Yes. I'm just resting," he calls up to me.

I ride the drum back, and as our group breaks up and begins to head out, I think of how full my hands are, how much I have to heal, and how tired Allusius and the others must be, watching over me.

 TWO ✪

I've become quite proficient at sliding through the portals, waiting every day for the time that I can come to the Dreaming. This is a daily ritual—visiting Simon, talking with him, even just watching him work his canvas.

He's working when I arrive, drawing at what looks like an old-fashioned inn keeper's desk. I peer down at his paper to see a simple black line drawing, only the lines move after he's drawn them. They keep moving, too, slip-knotting around each other, then releasing. He draws them with such a careful hand, yet they take their own form. As their artist, I'm not sure I could take their assertiveness so lightly, but Simon draws one line, then just goes on to the next.

I think to ask him why the lines behave that way, watching them wiggle into place, but something else comes to mind.

"Simon, can we talk a bit?"

He looks up and smiles, always pleased to see me. That in itself is an awesome feeling, to be greeted always with a smile.

"Of course," he says. I see that when he puts his stylus down, the lines settle into a tiny one-roomed cabin.

"I've been thinking about what Allusius said, about my hate, and I'm ready to do whatever I need to, or let you do whatever you need to do to heal this part of me. I know Allusius was right, and I can't keep feeling this way. I'll never heal while hating any part of myself."

He begins drawing again, but I have his attention.

"I'll face whatever I need to, do whatever I have to... Whatever admission, concession... *whatever I have to do.*"

He looks up from his drawing quite wistful, and I think for a minute that he will hug me. He doesn't and his wistfulness becomes disconcerting.

"What is it?" I ask.

"You have a very long history of being hurt by men."

He does hug me, but only after my legs have gone completely weak and I'm on the cold stone floor with him doting anxiously. I'm not sure how to describe having one's entire heritage so concisely summed up. It feels a lot like dizziness buzzing in my head, trickling warm and wet down my face and rushing down my body, hot and burning until my legs forget to stand and my knees smash into rock.

"That's why I chose you," he whispers, settling beside me on the floor, his arms coming around me. "I know what you've been through in this and other lives, and I want to be part of your healing."

When he says it, it's with such enthusiasm that I have to listen. I can't stay distracted with the thought looming that what happened to me in this life also happened in other lives, that this life wasn't the first time I was sexually assaulted, or the only time. I want to have his enthusiasm. I want to be able to learn truths, whatever they are, about my own spiritual past and still be passionate about healing it. Right now, his passion is going to have to suffice.

I wipe my face dry and look into his eyes, *really* look into them. They're just barely blue and so kind. Looking into them, I see that he's been waiting for me to ask for his help. He's been waiting for the opportunity to help me.

He stands, extending a hand to me. Everything is wobbly but with his help I manage to stand. Simon leads me away from his desk into a thicket of clouds. I know where we're going will be very dark as the clouds thin to sheer black. I'm guided only by the pressure of his hand on mine, his arm around my waist.

Wherever we are, we're not alone. A girl and a woman are with us. I wait for them to come into view, for the light to reveal where we walk, but the dark persists. The sounds of our tiniest movements echo in the enclosure, its emptiness dwarfed by the muffled security of my soft-soled shoes thumping across the hardwood floor. We stop in what I presume is the center of the room, and even though I still feel Simon's touch, I'm trembling.

"What's in the room, Simon?"

"Ask it," he whispers.

I call out, ask what, who is here. A booming voice replies, reverberating off what must be metal walls, so loud that I can't tell if it's male or female, just chaotic noise bouncing in my ears and head. The room is talking, and I feel it begin to close in tight around me. I still can't see, couldn't find my way out if I had to.

As the noise grows unbearable, the cool of metal presses into my bare arms. The din grows louder still, its vibration seeping from the confining walls into my already shaking body. I don't know what's happening or what this is. But I know I asked for it. I said I'd do anything, so I know this is *something*.

"What are you?" I whisper.

I hear wails in reply. It could be human, could be animal. I don't know, but it's unmistakably in agony. I think it's one voice. It could be many. The room amplifies with shrieks, then I hear a dense thud followed by a loud splintering. Pain bores into my skull and streaks down my spine. I feel like I'm running, making the motions, only I'm standing still pinned in place by this room. My mouth is clamped shut, teeth clenched into the meaty pulp of my cheek, yet I know I'm the one wailing. The taste of rust coats my tongue, oozing thick down my throat.

Something presses me down, holds me perfectly still as it rips into me, flesh yielding to heat tearing through me. From between my legs up to my navel my blood saturates me, warm, then cool, cold. I feel pressed flat on my back, yet I'm standing in this room, in the center of my own histories of rape.

It's pitch dark, but I know where Simon is, and I look in his direction. He tells me to continue, to trust my own healing intuition.

I have no intuition at the moment. All I have are words, so I say, "I know that you're part of me, and I need your help so that I can heal."

I mean what I say, and I know my words mean something to the room because the floor shakes with a rumble. I would have fallen, but the walls don't allow that much freedom of movement.

"You left me, and I hate you," the voice says.

Before I can process what it might be referring to, I hear, "Does that feel good?" It's a different voice in this tiny room somewhere with me, and I bristle. I know that voice.

"No," another voice says, a child's voice, mine. I can't run. I can't get out. I can't leave the room, can't breathe, and everything is pushing on me, crushing my chest, pressing my back flat and I can't... even... move.

"No?" he asks. I shake my head furiously, but the hands continue. They're on me as the floor continues to rumble.

I hate this. I hate this room, I hate being stuck, hate his hands on me, hate moving, hate breathing. If I can just be still enough, don't move, don't breathe, and he'll stop, he'll see that I really don't like it, and he'll stop.

Sweat beads my brow and my lungs burn until I'm forced to draw a breath from the stale metallic air. I can't stop breathing, panting, moving. I can't stop and I hate it, hate that I can't make him stop, hate my body for not doing what I want.

The room instantly fattens, and again I hit the floor, but no one rushes to console me. Still panting, I rise onto hands and knees, wondering where Simon is now, as my senses can no longer place him in the room.

I thought I was done with this, thought I'd left the self-destructive part of me in the flow charts of grief models, the behavior modification pro/con lists of my therapist. But I didn't. It's right here in this little room inside me, hidden away where I might never have found it without Allusius' revelation and Simon's direction. It's no wonder I stay sick with such a hateful place inside me.

I don't want to be here anymore, don't want it to *have to be* inside me anymore. It's a storage closet for holding onto how bodies respond to things they don't like, how mouths say "no" when feelings say "yes," where sickness grows up to mean "I hate you."

But this room is inside me, and it needs something from me as much as I need something from it. "I know we lied," I say, slowly rising to my feet. "What he did felt good, but you were just a little girl and he had no business touching me that way. You... I ...couldn't say no. And even when I did, he kept on anyway. He gave me no choice."

"I hated you." The voice is still loud but not unbearable.

"I hated you, too." It's true. I guess I'm my own contradiction: I'm the body whom I've hated for responding to his touch and the mind who despised the body's response.

"But I love you now, and I know that I won't be well unless you heal with me," I say. "You don't want to be what you've become and neither do I."

Now everything is quiet but not quite silent. I hear faint breathing, or maybe it's just my own.

"I'm afraid to feel," it says.

Without thinking, I blurt out, "And I'm afraid not to."

Something grasps my hand, and the room lights. Beside me stands a woman about my age, her left hand clasping my right. She's translucent and beautiful, my height, dressed in jeans and a fuzzy light blue sweater. Some seconds, she's a little girl in a tiny yellow frock, others a grown woman. The rest of the time, she's both at once. She doesn't have hair; rather, she has branches, some even with leaves still on them. I stare at her with my mouth agape, surely being rude, but she's the most exotic, beautiful thing I've ever seen and I can't take my eyes from her.

I know she's a soul part that has chosen to come back to me. She left in that moment under his hands, his body, when ideology clashed with sensation. Her hand warms mine, and it feels good. When I look down at our interlocked fingers, they've merged into one inseparable flesh. Yet her will hesitates in wanting to be with me. Her hesitation reminds me of the conundrum of the room: feeling just enough to discount what I've not wanted to feel.

"What do I need to do for you to come back with me? To stay with me now?"

I'm immediately taken back to a late night in college, a poet boy on the deck under the stars. My one hand has a beer; the other is clenched so tight my nails almost cut into my palm. Going there but not wanting to go there.

I always went there.

This girl's tried to come back to me many times, but my own behavior pre-empted her return. Even for myself, "no" had come to mean something other than "no." "No" had never meant "no," when I said it in childhood to him or even years later when I said it to myself.

Truly, I admire her fortitude in standing up for what she knows is right, even if I've had to live years without her, even if it has meant standing up to myself.

"I don't do that anymore," I tell her.

"I know," she says.

"I don't hate you anymore," I tell her. Something moves in me as I say the words, something heavy and cold being lifted out. It's just *gone...* an empty space left behind my belly button.

"I don't hate you, either."

"If you'll stay," I tell her, "I'll make sure that we are both well."

Simon comes then, instructing me to lie down and for her to lie inside me. In just that subtle merging of us, my senses awaken, sensations in my body that my mind attunes. I feel the pressure and movement of my clothes on my body, breeze flowing even through the tip ends of my hair. Simon's breath warms my solar plexus, then the crown of my head as he blows her back into me. The warmth spreads to my head and shoulders, through my hips and groin. But my solar plexus and second chakra grow hot where she settles, my belly tingling, that empty space filling with her.

I'm alive feeling her living in me, and for the first time that I can remember, I *like* the way feeling feels.

 THREE

"Simon." I lean on a cloud near his easel. "I'm really bothered that my family supports him. My father and his family open their homes to him, have him at their tables, yet they treated me so badly after I told them that he'd hurt me. I know it's their choice, and I respect that—I *really* do. But I'm hurt by it, and I just don't like feeling this way—stuck in the middle of respecting their choice but being hurt by it. How can I heal that contradiction?"

"There is no contradiction. Go with what you feel," he says, not looking up from his painting.

He makes more smudges of more colors that don't blend. I don't study his works anymore. I'm used to their subtle oddities now. I don't try to find secret messages in them or listen for them to speak. I just watch him work. That is the most beautiful part of his creations. I watch him paint and see how he gives his art the same attentiveness that he gives me. He chooses the colors carefully, always selective in the placement of his strokes, patiently smoothing the shiny paint across the waiting canvas. He creates what he wants, but the lively anomalies of his work are all their own. They do what they want. He would have it no other way. I watch Simon work and know that he allows me the same freedom.

But go with what I feel. Well, I feel more than one thing, that's the problem. My family's accusation of me when I told them what had happened made me feel like it was happening all over again, like I should have been able to count on them, be protected by them, trust them as I should have been able to trust him. And I should have told them how it made me feel when they blamed me. I should have…

Simon interrupts my thoughts, saying gently, "Don't try to fix it by blaming their reactions on what you *didn't* do. Just *feel* it."

I know what he means, to just sit with a feeling, acknowledge it. Don't try to change it or find a source for it. Don't analyze it. Just sit with it. One of the hardest things I've ever learned to do: picture myself, just sitting with feelings, feelings sitting with me, across a tiny floral tablecloth—a tea party. She takes sugar, but I drink mine straight, pinky down, a ritual we have honed over years, staring at each other, cups raised. The way other kids practiced a sport, learned a dance, I sat with feelings to learn who I am.

He's told me nothing I don't already know how to do, and this is a waste of my time. I set my teacup down indignantly, turning to him. "I *do* feel it, and I don't *like* it. I'm not trying to change how I feel or have you magickally make it stop hurting. *I want to resolve the problem.* I want peace. Why didn't deciding to stop seeing my family work? Why did my decision to sever those ties not resolve the fact that I wanted our family to be different, that I loved them? *How* can I love them when they have hurt me?"

I realize I've thrown a lot at him, and I'm wary of the possible outcome of a tantrum with a spirit guide. It's too late to take any of it back, and really, that's how I feel.

"We can never really cut off the souls of those who come into our lives," he says, looking at me pointedly. I feel no reproach in his tone or his gaze, but I look from him quickly, focusing again on his painting.

"I understand you," I say, backing away. He returns to his paints, and I pace behind him. When he dabs his brush on the border, I begin again.

"I'm not settling for that. I'm not a pawn of my karma. I'm a *maker* of it. If I choose to sever the spiritual connections to my abuser, then I'll do it. I harbor no malice for him, but he isn't welcome in my life to any degree, spiritual or otherwise, *anymore*. And at least for right now, *neither is our family who protects him."*

I stop pacing, facing him. He is beautiful when he paints. Like electricity on hot wires, the light gathers in the folds of his robes, dances over the creases of the fabric out his brush as it flies over the canvas. I admire him, though I'm still poised for his argument.

He says nothing, and his silence speaks more than I care to admit, a familiar grief knotting my chest. I should rise to something here, but instead I'm light-headed and need to sit down to steady myself

I blink, and we're in my Lower World. Allusius, Simon, the other animals who are teachers, helpers, and the powdery gold mist that I've come to know as my High Self hover near. We're huddled just beyond the pond at the base of the hill, and a light breeze moves wisps of clouds through sunny blue skies. It's any other day in my Lower World, except that my pulse and mind rage and we appear to be in deep thoughtful discussion, though I don't know about what.

Movement tiptoeing from the edge, a beautiful, unusually tall thin woman skulks from the middle of our horde. Slowly she moves, reflexes deliberate. She's pearly silver-green as are the wraps that she wears. Body spindly, she moves as if a constant unseen breeze flows through her, bending, bowing, rippling. She looks straight at me. In a flash she darts, the streamers of her dress trailing silver where she stood as she dashes toward the tree on the hill.

me.
I guard a tree
with wounded children in its
branches.
I give them
elevation

to dream.

She giggles into her palm as the words echo back to me. I roll them around as I see her step into the tree. I know my eyes are as big as Allusius' in his feather mask when I remember — I know those words! I wrote them a long time ago, and here that poem has just walked past me! She's a tree spirit, the dryad of the strange tree.

The leaves of the tree are a brilliant purple in the golden glow of the sunlight. She is illuminated, but the light rises from the apex of her branches, not from the sun. Directing my attention back to the pond, I notice silence around me as the discussion has stopped, and I stand alone by the water. If she is the part of me who creates dreams, maybe she has a dream for me?

Hand clasped over my mouth, I run to the tree. Nothing of her humanoid form shows except a face set in the trunk, perfectly still and solid, except for the eyes. I'm afraid to breathe as I take in her face. If I so much as move wrong, this may all blow away on a breeze, and I want to know about this tree.

I want to know how she came into my poem and my Lower World. Her eyes solidly fix on me, and her lips curl into a turned up smile. Her face is lined with dark pulpy rings, and I don't have to count them to know that she is very old. Moving closer, I peer into the strange elegant face. It blinks, smiles, studies my amazement. Apart from her facial movement, the only other signs of life are high in her halo of branches, all adorned with sleeping children shifting, laughing aloud, murmuring in their dreams.

She's exactly as I saw her in the poem, a vision from years before manifesting now. I never thought there could be such a tree, a safe place to rest, where I could dream all day and no one would think to look for me. So I wrote her into being. And now she's here. Hand still covering my mouth, I can only stare at her beauty.

I blink and it's dark. Things happen here so quickly! Stars sparkle through her leaves when I look up, and a moon hangs low behind the sleeping forms in her branches.

"What insight do you have about these feelings for my family?"

A haze surrounds me as I stand before her, and I'm not sure of where I'm standing anymore. Hugs smother me from arms that I don't see, just feel. Hugs that don't let go though I pull away press in, then tickling that isn't the least bit funny lingers with the feeling that something is coming.

I shudder to think what that is, but I hope it's the good kind of hug or maybe just some rest. Maybe I don't have to dream. I'll just rest, sleep for once, without nightmares.

I look around and see that I'm alone except for the dryad. Even her crown of children is now gone, leaving plenty of room for a new boarder. Sighing, I stretch, grasp a lower branch, and lift myself from the ground.

The smooth gray bark is cool under my hands, scraping lightly against my knees. Easily, I climb limb to limb, and I remember this! I remember tree houses, falling and getting right back up with only the thought of climbing higher. I remember battlements made of blankets, the saving grace of being hidden high in leaves, and the knapsack-tablecloth-Kool-Aid parties hosted on their roots. I'd forgotten how remarkable climbing trees is!

I'm high up now but close to her center, and I'm afraid of neither falling to the ground nor being so close to the sky. Curled on my side, I face into her trunk while all around me, she is secure, stable.

Quickly I am the dream as well as the dreamer watching it unfold. I see a beach with my young father throwing a volleyball to me. I catch it, the cool water swirling over my ankles as I run through the surf. When I throw it back, from the corner of my eye I see someone's coming. There's a figure, foggy in the distance, walking, coming straight toward me, growing taller as it approaches.

It's a young man in shorts, a collared shirt, loafers, no socks. I look back for my father, but he's gone. There is only me, the beach, and the man coming.

He grows familiar as he approaches, and I see that it's my father, younger than I've ever known him, but him. He's in his teens, maybe early twenties. He's young, and I sense him to be naive but receptive, eager. I don't know why he's coming and I'm paralyzed, thinking back to that beckoning look the dryad gave me earlier, knowing that she put me in this dream. The only coherent thought my mind forms is wondering if I would hear her limbs crashing to the ground over roar of a chainsaw. This isn't the dream I thought I was giving up my reality for.

My father and I stare for a long while, not uncomfortable, but not fulfilling our reason for coming to the Dreamtime, either.

"I'm sorry." He says it over and over, and something inside me breaks, streams down my face. In my slumber, I wipe my face, my other hand gripping the cool bark beneath me.

It's sincere, more so than anything he's ever said to me, but I flash to this young version of him holding me right after I was born, cradled in warm blankets. This is the first time in this life that he's held me. The antiseptic of the hospital stings my nose as I see tiny hands strain toward his face. He's proud, and he makes a silent promise of redemption to himself for things that aren't mine to know. He's consumed with wanting to *do it right* this time, with the idea that with this child he can make things as they should be, though I don't know exactly what he sees as wrong.

I only sense that my birth was his last recognition that he was spiritually off-track, and I sense that my birth was not as significant to him as seeing me as his last hope for salvation.

In the tree, I roll onto my other side and years pass. He's broken, leaving our home, cowering under the weight of expectation, failure, lost youth. He's thinking of nothing, no one, as he throws his clothes into a black plastic bag. He's forgotten everything, even his chance at redemption, and he has no love in him for anyone, just a void.

Leaves and twigs scrape my back as I shift into knowing that my father didn't love me, himself, or anyone else, and for that time, he could not.

Yet here on the beach, this young part of him loves me and always has. This soul aspect is part of what he was trying to get back to, to make his life right. I see this aspect of him standing on the sideline of my father's life even now, rooting for him, for us to finally have a loving relationship.

We can never really cut off the souls of those who come into our lives.

"I accept your apology," I tell him. "Please accept mine for not knowing how else to deal with you and your actions." His arms surround me, a perfectly fitted hug, affirming that we can meet in love if not in waking, in the Dreaming. And as rare as it is for people to sincerely apologize for the hurts they commit, I'll accept the apology without question, even if it can't actually come from his waking aspect.

The tide rises, falls, and we sit on the beach holding hands. Not talking, no real need to talk, just enjoying the breeze, the sun, the uniquity of this visit.

I awaken to darkness and the sting of bark impressions on my face. Carefully, I creep through the branches and snake down the trunk. Looking into the dryad's face, she smiles, knowing the dream that I found in her.

"Thank you," I say.

She doesn't speak, but the invitation is extended — I feel it. Someday, I'll dream with her again. She'll bring me another dream as helpful as this one.

I descend the hill looking out over the landscape that has slowly filled, become more vivid with each journey. An odd procession of glowing creatures, animals, people, my spirit family follows me to my portal, bidding me farewell.

Just at the cave opening, I pause and ask, "Will you come back with me, into waking?" I've wanted to ask them for a long time, but it never felt quite right. I figured that was because I wasn't ready. But I'm ready now. I hope they are.

Without another word, first Allusius, then Simon steps into my body. When they settle, I feel them breathe when I breathe, move when I move. When I speak, I have their insight bolstering the words coming out of my mouth, their input on my intentions behind the words. I carry their best and highest attributes with me. We walk back into the forest, toward waking, to here, where when I sit up out of this journey. I don't see them with my naked eye; I know they're with me. I know they love me.

 FOUR

She's come again.

Rather, Simon's taken me to her again.

"I stay sick all the time, lately," I told him. "Can you take me to someone who can help me heal any remaining issues connected to these urinary tract infections, so that I can finally let go of them?"

And so here she is: ugly, old, short, and bent over. A Crone as I live and breathe, complete with stringy white hair and bluish complexion. She's not at all the woman that I met originally, not the angel that I thought she was, and certainly not the goddess whom I sought to heal me.

The first time I met her was when I'd asked Simon a desperate question, something about my relationship and pulling it out of the fire.

He'd taken me to a courtyard at a high level of my Upper World, a garden with sculptures, flowers, vines connecting ground to stone such that everything seemed alive, moving. She was pretty then, if you can say things like that about goddesses. Stern, fixed stare, at least eight feet tall, perfectly fair skin, dark blue and crimson robes. I revered her with more respect than anything in my life, and she probably commanded it more than anything else ever had. Although I was eternally grateful for the knowledge she'd imparted to me that day, I wasted no time returning to waking. She left me reeling with awe.

The second time I met with her, I had summoned her out of anger.

My life had spun out of control, and I demanded no less than her energy to tame it. I called to her, not even knowing who she was, yet fully knowing that summoning deities in this manner wasn't very smart. But she came, angry and foreboding. She even gave me what

I sought, and I left humbled, understanding that I was to call on her any time I needed her intervention. I didn't know to what I owed that great favor given my impudent behavior. But her wrath left me so rattled that I vowed never to call on her again and to never act in such haste, regardless of the state of my life.

I never intended to see her again, but Simon has brought me here. Before, she looked nothing like the stooped hag that she is now, but I know she's the goddess from the other journeys. They are one and the same.

Simon says she's a new guide, but I'm not in the market for a new one. I like Simon quite well, and I tell him this. I tell him, "Thank you, but no thanks."

"She has things you have need of learning, things that are not mine to teach you. I will remain with you always, but you must walk with her for now."

He says she's a goddess, and that she is me, pre-Celtic but spanning many cultures, many eras. She is powerful and god-like, of that I have no doubt. I've felt her incredibly stunning energy, both alluring and terrifying. I feel it now, and it's very foreign to me. It's not me. It's nothing I want to be part of I have enough conflicting feelings without inviting more.

"I don't understand what you mean, that she is me," but he doesn't clarify, just steps back until there are only clouds where he stood.

Now I'm alone with her, and I have no idea what to do. She doesn't move to do anything. I'm not even sure she's paying attention to me as she seems to be in a daze with her hands held up, palms facing out. She looks past her hands into nowhere.

I stand back, taking in this new form. Her aura is bright blue and is the only light emanating from her black robes and blue-ash skin. I don't feel that she is good or bad, which is quite disconcerting because everyone

I've met in the Dreamtime up until this point has been fairly clear cut in their intentions. I can't easily dismiss her, yet I can't accept her. I impede myself, and I don't know why. All I know is that in her presence, I panic, and I know that's a reflection on me more than on her.

She turns away, and when she faces me again, she's a beautiful woman. Even her energy is different now, gentler and I don't know why how I see her affects my feelings about her. Don't care to, really, and I've grown tired of observing. I just want answers.

"What do I need to do differently to heal this part of my life?"

"Love you," she says. She smiles when she says it, which is really strange, considering she was a menacing hag a minute ago. I want to mock her sincerity but can't. Either way, she tells me nothing I don't already know and have been joyfully calling back into my life for months now.

"What else?" I ask.

"Nothing. I am healing you. There is nothing for you to do."

Passive healing. That's a new concept. I don't know what she's doing, but even as she speaks, I feel better, healthier. She moves in front of me and dips her hands into my body, tugging, shifting, moving things around, then turns me as a seamstress would turn her model, smoothing out a good fit at each stop. I'm safe in her care, and under her touch, my body calms.

I don't know who she is or what she wants. And even though she frightens me, my life is better when she's here. I always leave her presence *well*. So I'll accept her gift. I'll let this happen. I can let someone else do the healing *for* me for a change.

Five

Simon and Allusius keep dropping books, and I keep picking them up, filing them away in various body parts. When I put the books inside me, I know they settle into my chakras first. In my spine, a warm glow begins, then emanates throughout my body all the way to my fingertips and toes. I can't read the books, but I wrote them. They tell me that I wrote them.

The books are leather bound, dusty, thick heavy pages that are handwritten, hand drawn images. Some are loose pages that waft from the sky, leaves from the heavens. They're all vaguely familiar, but nothing I can identify. Every one of them is important, and I can't read any of them.

Tough love guides, I have. Allusius and Simon are quick to offer comfort, protection, love. But they push me to my own conclusions. I ask them to help me iron out my wrinkles, they hand me a crumpled page. I ask them to teach me to read the books, I get a torn manuscript. I ask them to read the books to me, they leave me standing alone with pens and paper. I yell, scream, cry; a book falls from out of nowhere.

So I place the books in my body, knowing they're mine to have, to keep, hoping to gain their insight. Yes, cosmic osmosis: diffusion of wisdom into a soul. How ironic that I'm a writer, and lately I can't write even one word, string together a coherent thought, let alone a creative one. Then, in the Dreamtime, I can't even read.

In waking, my head hurts too badly to read or write or much else. It's hurt for nine months straight, and my doctors don't know why or how to make it stop. It started about the time this goddess came in. I haven't seen her much, but I feel her, the absent healing that she's doing in my soul. In spite of her work, my body seems sicker. I keep thinking maybe the cure is in the books, and if I hold onto them long enough, the books will either hasten the healing this goddess brings me or I'll figure out what they say.

I ask Simon what I need to do about the books and the headaches, and he says, "Leave your job." He says it simply, in the true spirit of us lounging lazily against this log at the bottom of the dryad's tree.

Would that spending all day leaning on this log talking with him afforded me the same life as my fairly well-paying position as a technical writer! This approach of reckless abandon is in keeping with the responses I've been getting from him about everything lately. I ask him if I'm in the career that will fulfill my life purpose, and I hear, *shaman*. I ask him what I should be doing, I hear *shaman*. How this relates to illness, books, and the resolution being to leave my job, I don't know.

"I know you see the bigger picture, but I don't, and I can't just leave my job." I roll my eyes, laugh casually, trying to ignore the ache in my chest, the knowledge that I'm supposed to be doing something more here. My stomach churns knowing that I'm not doing it.

"I have no big aspirations of wealth, but I would like to keep a roof over my head, and I need an income to do that."

"I will provide," he says, thoughtfully rubbing a blade of grass between his thumb and forefinger. He studies the blade intently. It's the brightest of green, new, all the seasons ahead of it, but nothing really intriguing comes from my examination of it or of his fascination with it.

Pulling back from the distracting blade, I goad him. "But I don't see *how*. How do I make that kind of transition? Just leap out of a job into some scattered pages of shamanism? If that's providing, I'm going to have migraines for a long time."

He stares at me intently, and my head throbs with the pain I've had for the last nine months.

"I don't even feel safe journeying. The fevers I've had with the headaches and all the medicine I've taken have left me loopy, and I don't even trust my own judgment right now, which means, I don't trust my intuition, and that's just a shortcut to depression."

He focuses again on the blade in his fingers, his other hand absentmindedly plucking another from the ground. His gaze shifts to the new blade, unfazed by my rant.

"I grew up sick, on purpose, because sick meant safe. It meant home, and someone would finally look after me. I don't feel safe right now, and I haven't all these months, and frankly, it's very *comfortable*. I can't afford to go back to those ways now."

Silently I beg him to speak to me, show me something, give me a feeling to *know*. His gaze merely goes from one blade of grass to the other.

"Simon, why now that I've made the conscious choice to heal myself and help other people has my body and my life fallen apart?"

He lays the blades casually back on the ground. "Where you are going, you can bring nothing with you."

For a split second, I stare at him with my mouth open. When I blink again, I'm standing on a dirt path in the woods with a suitcase in each hand. Then mysteriously, the suitcases disappear, even the overcoat I'm wearing vanishes...and my shoes!

Somehow I understand from that silly visual that he doesn't just mean I don't get to bring a toothbrush on my travels. I don't get to bring my pain, my past, my expectations, my insecurities, or the illnesses of my past.

I blink again and I'm back on the hill. He looks at me firmly, with a hint of sadness. Simon has chosen these words carefully, and I know they're his blessing words, his initiation words to me. They are the words that give significance to this illness and shine light on where it's leading me.

To be free of the things I've been lugging through life sounds fantastic! I know I can't possibly envision the things Simon sees coming, but just the possibility of being able to heal *all* of me makes whatever is behind the serious expression he's wearing worth it.

I want to say more, to ask him more about where I'm going, but I don't think I want to know. I don't want to be *told*. I want to just live it. Even though I can't exactly see the destination, I know the getting there is going to feel much better than where I've been so far.

My destiny is under my control, shaping it with my own hands. I'll never be able to reach out to anyone or anything else in my life if I can't travel light. I have to let go of everything I think I know in order to heal, or I'll never be able to read those books my guides give me. I'll never be able to write them.

Plucking a blade of grass, I twirl it between my thumb and forefinger, looking over the meadow of my Lower World, resolving that I can start over again, beginning now.

Six

They're here again, that tribe. I don't know exactly what tribe they are, but they're South American. I've been seeing them when I journey lately.

I'm not alarmed, which at first was very alarming. I didn't ask them in, so I don't know how they got here. Perhaps I did ask them in, and I haven't remembered doing so yet. Maybe they've always been here and I just wasn't seeing them. I'm comfortable in their presence, like I'm one of them. The men stop what they're doing and nod when I pass. I try to help with their work, but the women take chores from me, bring me fruits and breads, delicious meats cooked over open fires.

They respect me for a reason I don't know. They don't say or do anything in particular, but they treat me like it's an honor. Like they were waiting for the opportunity of our meeting. I'm uncomfortable with that sort of flattery. I'm uncomfortable with *any* sort of flattery. I don't like drawing attention at all; that it could be positive is an afterthought.

This log has come to be a regular meeting place for Simon and me. It's out of the way, to one side of the valley yet close enough to observe the tribe in their daily routine. We sit beside each other watching them prepare a huge bonfire.

"Simon, they treat me like I'm a person of influence among them. It makes me uneasy, and I enjoy their company too much to remain uncomfortable around them. Maybe I'm being ungrateful, but I just want to be one of them. I don't want to be set apart for any reason."

"You already are," he replies.

The air between us is thick enough that my breath sticks in my throat, and I wheeze. My attention is fully on him as he looks back at me, expressionless. The knowledge that I'm different somehow doesn't set well with me, though I'm comforted by his confidence.

The tribe pulls me into their huddle around the fire. I'm dully pale next to their dark skins. Their white teeth and opalescent eyes glow in the flickering blaze. Even their coal-black hair casts a blue aura in the soft light. They emanate light themselves, contrasting with their dark features. Each of them has some article of clothing or other adornment on their person that's a pretty bright blue.

Wrapped in loose blankets, they bring skins with thick fur to clean, branches to carve into pipes as we settle around the fire.

One of the women brings me a book, and they all press in around me—adults, youth, elderly holding infants. I sense their waiting, wanting, like sleepy children milking more from a bedtime story. I begin reading to them in this strange language that I don't know.

From the first paragraph, impressions come, foggy familiarities. Shocked, I realize I'm reading of my life. Yule mornings wading through mountains of crackling wrapping paper in footed pajamas, deaths of loved ones and the horrible speeches people offer in funeral processions to try and comfort, and loves so intense they're aeons of seconds with joy and sadness all at once.

The book tells of things before I was now, before I was me. As I read, I'm looking down over my life in words, seeing it spelled out like it hasn't happened yet. Even the pages themselves are alive, living, turning themselves, urging me to keep reading to the tribe. Moving illustrations speak, turn on the page to wave at us, people that I recognize from my life, and some that I don't but feel fondly for.

All through the events of my life, the tribe feels them with me, leaning over my shoulders, pointing and laughing at the lively pictures, other times weeping quietly with me, the soft hide of a wrap caressing my skin as someone rubs my back. They have the same intuitive connection to the book that I do, seeing its whimsical display. Yet, a voice inside me that they don't hear, the voice of the book says, *There's more to come. It's coming. It's here.*

As it speaks, I realize that with this book, I've more than chronicled the events of my life or transcribed a message for some unseen force. I've studied, consulted, acted in the roles. I've *lived* the message that's written in this book, one that I'm now reading to others.

I look up from the pages, and I'm not reading anymore. I stand alone at the fire. After a few seconds, a young man comes, his hand extended, and he leads me deep into the woods. He's tall, dark-skinned, black hair, light eyes, wears only a breechcloth. In a white gown, I too am dark with black hair. I realize quickly that we're not only walking deeper into the forest, but back in time, to an ancient people, to the First Tribe, to humanity, before The Fall. I watch him go, leading, parting brush for me to pass, and as he turns to hold the path clear for me, I see that he has Simon's eyes.

Drums, hundreds of them, are pounding, hypnotic. Their cadence is my pulse, my mind is flashes of blue bodies blurring around flames.

Thickets part to a level grass circle. The tribe dances there, more nude than clad. Their bodies are explosions of a bright blue substance. Hundreds of them dance, circling a great fire. They slow as we approach, parting to enclose us within their throng. With the persistent drumming and rattling, the dance resumes and they surround me as the heat of their bodies and the element envelops us.

They show me the motions of their ghost dance, and I begin circling the fire with them. As I become lost in the rhythm of the drum, dizziness overcomes me and my eyelids grow heavy. I grow distant from my body. The man with Simon's eyes suddenly emerges from the throng almost nose-to-nose with me, his heavily lidded whites stark against the blue substance he now wears.

Powder is blown into my face, and I'm outside myself, bright blue scattering over my whole body in that one *poof*, wild in my hair, streaking my face. As the powder settles on me, I'm outside myself seeing the whites of my eyes glow in the frame of blue powder and black hair. I see also that I'm the only one in a white linen gown, the only one dressed at all.

Dancing and swaying, hands move over me, around me. I look down to see my gown change to silvery white, luminescent like the robe that appears on me when I work in the sandy medicine circle of my Lower World. The gown is soft silver, like Simon's robes.

The tribesman leads again and I follow. We climb, emerging high above my Upper World. We move up above the clouds where there are forms in clusters, creatures bent over, working intently. I move closer and see that workers are hunched over disembodied human parts. There's no blood and no discernible wounds on the severed parts, although my logical mind tells me that there should be. I don't even sense that they have any pain. It's just upsetting to me, seeing body parts carefully laid out on tables. Everyone here, even the tribesman, seems unfazed by this place, but I panic and want to leave.

I don't see any way out. I wouldn't know the way back if I tried, but I don't think I'm supposed to be here. I shouldn't be seeing this. Yet compelled, I can't help but watch the workers re-assembling, waking, animating the forms lying in front of them. Even when there's only a head and leg connected, they sit up, talk, move around.

One of the strange patients looks over the shoulder of its worker at me and smiles. It should be chilling, gruesome, even, but I'm surprisingly calm and elated as I realize what this is: This place is where we're made. This place is where our souls are cleansed and healed, prepared to return to Earth, and this creature in its purest form is receiving life, fulfilling its choice to be reborn.

Not only are the patients ecstatic with their making, but the happy workers labor with careful hands and the purest of intentions. There is no negativity in them at all as they assemble these *soulbodies*.

As I watch them work, I remember their hands touching me, wiping away my fear and self-consciousness, soothing me back to the womb. And I remember the presence that is Simon with me then as he walks with me now.

I look over at the tribesman who has Simon's eyes, and I wonder about him then. Just how long have I known him, how many lives have we walked together? I think of all the wonderful things he's seen in his time, and I feel like a child playing dress up.

I'm standing here in an angel's gown, smeared with screaming blue powder. I know I'm a sight, all wild hair and smudges, standing by perfect creatures making *soulbodies*, who are perfect creatures in their own right. Among them, I'm self-conscious, and I focus really hard on being wallpaper, just watching them work.

As I observe, one of the workers turns to me, placing a cool hand over mine, giving me a warm smile. The *soulbody* on which it works cranes its head to look directly at me. It's quite plain, yet radiantly beautiful at the same time. It has no discernible facial features other than tiny black dotted eyes, its body mostly shapeless glowing white light, and the occasional limb or ear. All thoughts of my appearance and naïveté, of clinging to the shadows flee, and I step up to the beautiful form in awe. I take its hand as it's being prepared, wondering who it will be, who it is, and if I'll recognize it when we meet in waking.

The tribe has something to do with my ability to see this creature being made. They have awakened something in me with their dance and blue powder, and showing me this creation place for souls is some part of it. I don't know what it is, I'm only eternally grateful to share this experience with this *soulbody*.

The tribesman gestures, and I follow him into the clouds. He stops short, and I go on ahead knowing he's following. More clouds enfold me, and although I can't see, I know where we are, where he has quite passively led me. We enter the garden where I met the goddess, with its cool damp grass, flowers newly bloomed. Stone steps rise in the garden's middle, and I am compelled to go to them.

She's there, the guide that Simon has impressed upon me, standing on the pedestal at the top of the steps, waiting. I have kept her at the edge of influence, held at bay. Different still from the last time I saw her, she's a saint, powerful, more so than ever. The closer I get to her, I feel her, I'm drawn. I can no longer doubt that she is a goddess, an archangel, a warrior of the light. I'm in awe of her beauty and power, which are far more compelling than the fear that had gripped me on our previous visits.

She's more human-seeming now, older, plumper. Slowly, I look up at her from her dainty satin clad feet to her hands clasped in prayer position at her heart, all the way up to her hair, which is covered by a habit forming her face into a round pale moon. As I study her porcelain features, she releases her hands and a book falls from her middle. Her features fade until she's gone, but the book continues to fall in slow motion, gold pages bound in bright blue leather tumbling into my hands.

I gather the book and hold it close, trying to read the page to which it has fallen open. It's handwritten, colorful images, but its message remains a mystery. Closing it, I run my fingers over the plain cover, where a title should be. Sequentially, I thumb through the pages of strange writing, baffled. It's much like the book I read to the tribe earlier, yet I can't read it. But it's mine, and I place it in my middle, a blue smudge remaining on my gown after it has disappeared in my solar plexus.

I step from the clouds into my Lower World, and I'm me, regular hair, regular jeans, and t-shirt. Simon is himself, yet for some reason, it's difficult to actually *see* him. Squinting, I see him in khaki pants, then a kimono, blonde hair, then red. I realize for the first time how utterly bizarre it is to notice more of him than just face and hands or to see him take on different forms.

Curious, I say, "Show me your body."

His robe parts to reveal swirls, brilliant colors, like one of his paintings. There are living creatures in there, yet nothing that has words to name it. There's no body for his head to rest upon, no torso for his hands to attach to.

I study his eyes closely, the one feature of him that I have always recognized. I understand that I see of him what he shows me. I see of him what I need to see, which at the moment is a kaleidoscope of colors morphing, joining, expanding. However I see him, it doesn't change how I've always known him to be. Staring into the swirling colors of my guide, I know that as long as I know what the books say, the skill of reading them is moot.

I thank him for this journey, silently thank the tribe for this initiation. As I make my way back to the portal, I hear drumming in the distance, my arms moving in time to the beat, the rhythm and motion of the ghost dance carrying me back to waking.

SEVEN

"I have no intention this time, Simon. I just need to be here. I'm not coping well anywhere else."

As has become par, I follow him into the woods, where we lie down and sleep. I awaken without him, and the tribe of blue people is standing over me.

I realize I've been accepted as part of the tribe for a long while now, but something is different this visit. A group of women pull me aside and into a hut. They make me up, painting my face an opaque white. The only color remaining is the blue of my irises and tiny black pupils. With gentle fingers, bright blue feathers are placed in my hair line framing my face, not just resting there, but becoming my hair. I brace for the blood that is sure to trickle from their insertion. None comes, only warm tingles that emanate through my scalp where the quills pierce. The women are solemnly silent as they work, finishing by wrapping me in a cloak of feathers.

My belly is silver white, bright blue feathers border, speckling my back. I am transformed, a new creature, an owl. Nothing in me remains human.

An elder comes, perhaps a medicine man, chanting over me in a strange tongue. I don't know what he speaks, but I know that he's bringing me more than just into the tribe, he's making me into something *for* the tribe, and for my life.

He finishes, and we sit facing each other across a small fire. "What's your name?" I ask. He doesn't answer, but I see that his eyes are Simon's, and I leave it at that.

I don't understand their want of me or what I'm to do, but whatever it is, I want to do it, and I want to do it right. I feel that he is waiting for me to put something into motion, but first things first.

"I've been remade," I begin. "Who am I?"

He tells me several names, and my own, information I've been told before, yet it's not entirely familiar. Then he continues, saying something completely new.

"You are the spokesperson of a People."

"What people?"

"The People Of The Sun."

"Who are these People?" He doesn't respond. Instead, he stands and begins dancing, chanting and rattling circles around me. He tells me that I'm protected, that I've always been protected, and when he says it, it's true. In spite of the events of my childhood, I've always felt that I was looked after — another paradox I've never been able to rationalize.

"I will present many pathways to you, to move you to where you can best speak this message," he says.

"What message?"

The elder places his hand over my third eye, and I gradually feel weightless, detached from my body. I don't even feel the pressure of his hand anymore, though I know it's still on my brow.

From behind my closed lids and his hand, I see myself standing at the base of a wooded hill. It's twilight and I'm alone in the forest, soon to be alone in the *dark* forest. I hear the shrill call of a hawk somewhere above, the scuffling of animals through the leaves and grass of the forest floor. Bigger, more powerful animals look from hiding places in the woods, yet I'm not afraid. I know nothing of looking after myself in this wild place, what direction to go in, how to feed or find water, but I know that I'll be all right.

Venturing up the hill, I make my way to its top where I look out over lesser hills. I sense life there, human, though it's not a place that I've seen before, and I don't actually see anyone.

In my mind, I ask the elder if I'm seeing what I need to see in order to know the message he speaks of. After a few seconds of silence, I turn to walk back down the hill, but the elder is now standing beside me.

Moving behind me, he turns me to face out over the valley, placing both hands over my eyes. In a few seconds, I begin to see people scurrying through their daily lives, carrying bundles home from the market, children playing with animals in the worn dirt path. On a distant ridge, there is a bear eagerly watching a group of men build a stone dwelling. Careening off the bear's ridge, a form flies toward us, growing monstrously huge. I freeze, afraid to move more from fear of disturbing its flight than for my safety. This creature, a winged reptile, flies mere feet in front of us.

I would have never thought this valley sustained such life. And from mere looking across the landscape, it doesn't. He's shown me another way to see the life in things.

"How do I change my life, my profession to make room for this message?"

"You will know how when the situation presents itself."

I ask him if there is more that I need to know about this message, and he says, "You will do fine."

I know he's shown me a wonderful thing and given me great promise in my own life. But how do I rise to this? How does he know I'm the person for this? I trust what he says. I have no reason not to. Somehow I'll know what to do and when to do it. I just wish that I had all of the answers now.

"You will finish something you started long ago," he says as if reading my thoughts. "Know that you have complete freedom not to take this task. You are *free* and ever loved, no matter what you choose. You do not have to do anything you don't want to. You are your own master. You are not indebted to this People. The tribe is indebted to you. Eventually, you will come to overshadow them, and it will be right."

My mind is boggled by all he is telling me, and my immediate response is to put my face in my hands and cry. I'm free to choose and still be loved? Protected, regardless of my choice? I can do whatever I want with my life and lose none of the spiritual guidance and protection they give me, even if I choose to walk away from it all? He presents me not only with a task, but with a new peace. I've never been offered love without strings before. And until this moment, I never understood the element of choice in truly being loved.

When I look up from my hands, there's smoke, choking, blowing in my face through the tribesman's pursed lips. Through the smoke, I see a boy, almost a man. It is I, dark skin, long black straight hair braided down my back. He wears leggings of skin and a colored woven shirt made by someone who loves him. This young man, I, stand alone on a plain in the western United States, staring up at a bright full moon. This place is not his home but a scared space of his people. He's not far from his tribe as I see hills with dwellings in the distance.

I've made camp consisting of a throw to sleep on, basic utensils, and tools. There is no food, only water. I see him, myself, staring at the moon, taking it in as the moon speaks to him. Something, someone beyond the moon, is talking, saying things that only he can hear, things that were his life purpose to pass on to his tribe. Breathing in this shaman's smoke, I hear those words from the moon though they are in a language that, in this life I don't know, though on the plain I listen intently.

The vision quest has been given. Born a member of this tribe and now reborn into them, I receive this initiation as spokesperson from their elder as I once received the call of the moon.

Heat rises from my body, and I look down to see a glow floating around me. So much to process, but before the elder, I'm calm, resolute. New life hums under my skin, and I feel every feather in my body stretch wide as I rise and fly into the night, to the moon.

It's on feet that I land in the meadow with Simon. His eyes speak to me, echoing something I've heard before, something someone told me or perhaps something I once said. This experience, seeing this past...it feels so real, but I need to hear it from him. I need to hear Simon's truth of this initiation.

"Who am I? What's my spirit name?"

He says exactly what the elder did, names that I can only tell a select few in my life.

Squinting at him, I sense this new guide, the tribe, and the initiation are all related, but I don't know how or if that relationship is important. I feel and honor the truth of it and, at the same time, am overwhelmed with the loss of not having known this information for years, even lifetimes.

"Who are you?" I ask.

"I am your guardian." He says it, and I know there have been lives with him, pasts and futures, some in bodies, others only as souls. But always, in every one of them, he was there, and I was protected. I still don't understand or can't let myself I ask him what I am.

Shaman, I hear many voices say at once, *writer, lover, Goddess, teacher*.

I hear these words, and I know they should bring some kind of relief, to finally have *someone* say it, spell it all out for me. I still feel like a child playing dress up.

I don't know what it means or what I'm supposed to be. I find myself crying again, unsure of what to do next.

"You have no more past to heal," Simon says, his hand resting lightly on my shoulder. Looking down at my body, I notice that a blue grid surrounds it. I've seen this grid before when I look for the source of illness in myself and others, a cosmic x-ray that is the life force in and around the body. I've never seen one that looks as mine does now. Examining the grid closely, I see that nothing is broken, sick, or hurt—body, mind, soul, or emotion. I see that I am well.

"Being *healed* doesn't mean you are finished," he says. "It means that you are no longer lost to pain or sickness. It means that you have access to all the knowledge that you need to heal anything about yourself now, which includes knowing when to reach outside yourself to someone else for help. Being healed means committing to use your resources and knowledge. This knowledge is healing. This knowledge makes your life now new."

Stock still, I'm in disbelief, even though I know Simon has always been honest with me. He's telling me that my chronic illnesses have cures if I really want to do what it will take to heal them, that my pasts of pain have joy if I'm willing to examine them to find it, that I have turned away the aid of a new guide who has come to try to help me with all of these things.

"Why was I made an owl?" I ask him.

"Walking with the owl lets you see inside creatures to know what needs healing. And with the strong wings of an owl, you can carry the souls of the dead to Spirit."

He stops there, though I sense that there's more he wants to say. He doesn't have to. I know what he isn't saying. Very kindly, Simon's telling me that with all that has come to pass and all the help that has been made available to me, the only thing standing in my way now is me.

EIGHT

I've not been here in a couple of months, but it's still my beautiful valley, my lively stream and rippling pond. It's still safe, home.

I'm not sick anymore, and I've begun feeling comfortable with the idea of working with others on a spiritual level. My life is becoming everything I thought I wanted in my healing, yet I'm paused. Even as I stand here on the slope, my feet are rooted, like they don't really want to move. I don't know when I became so afraid of moving.

I close my eyes and ask, "What's the source of this anxiety?" to no one in particular.

The words go before me and I follow them, opening my eyes to a crowd of sickly pale and needy faces. I'm pale myself and with red hair. The ground is cold and muddy beneath my feet. I'm dressed in a plainly colored chemise and bodice. The faces all wait in a line to see me, and I put my hands on each one of them, reading their illnesses and telling them how to heal themselves. And much later, in this cold place, I die and my body burns just above their upturned smiles and thankfulness.

Next I'm young, dark-skinned, in Africa where it's warm and there's no need for a lot of clothes. The people in this place need help, and after they've learned how to heal themselves, we dance drenched, thanking the rain.

Then I'm uniformed, a nurse maybe, a woman running across a moor, panting not from lack of breath but from the suffocation of fear as a huge army crests the hill behind me. There's a man with eyes that I recognize but can't place. The hooves of his horse pound beside me reverberating with the fear in my chest. Arms grab me, push me down, pinning me to the ground with a blade.

Bones separate. Blood seeps into the ground until I'm no longer this woman, but am fear, withholding, denial.

A shift, and I'm another young woman, in a white gown, lying on the floor of a bare room. This vision is from a recent era. I see running water, though the room is candlelit. She's locked in this place because of visions and voices. They think she'll hurt herself or someone else.

At night, creatures that she can't see taunt her, much as her keepers torment her during the day. No one believes the things she sees, the voices she hears. When one of her keeper's head turns, in a split second of freedom, she's running, then plummeting to the bottom of a cliff, hitting the rocks where the water breaks along with her body. In her last thoughts, I hear promises of never coming back here to this kind of life again.

Night comes in a different place, bringing stars, and I'm an old woman with an owl familiar on my shoulder. This is an old time, before history was written. There's a lush green valley, mountains, and a waterfall, and this is her home though I don't recognize the place. This vision feels the same as when I saw that young man on the plain talking to the moon, but I'm her with the owl, here, with the same intent listening to the night sky.

The scene shifts subtly, and I'm not her. I'm just watching her from the bushes nearby, this old, hard, shadow-veiled woman in this beautiful place. Her stiff white hair sprouts in tufts beneath her cowl, and I know her. She is the guide still waiting for me to call her in, and she's colored blue, the tribe's blue, in and all around her. I know this blue is a connection to the tribe, though she is not their ethnicity, their culture. This crone scares me, and I think I've done something wrong for this dark creature to have chosen to watch over me. I don't understand how *she* could be a guide for me.

She's looking up, and I follow her gaze to the blue light hovering above the mountain. No other animal or creature in the vale sees it but her and me, and I want to ask what it means, who she is, who I am to her. I want not to be afraid and step out of the bushes, but the wind is blowing, pushing me far from the valley until I'm not there. I'm not anywhere, and screaming, I beg Simon to find me.

Silence. Again there is stillness, and I open my eyes to see that I'm still standing on my slope. I never left it, rooted in place and surrounded by the quiet, peaceful warmth of my Lower World. In the silence, I know that these visions were all me, the lives, the pain, the ecstasy, the deaths. What started as lives as a healer, turned into repressed abilities and insanity, a thread that's woven itself even into this life.

A hand gently squeezes my shoulder. Simon.

Without even looking at him, I ask, "What else do I need to know about feeling persecuted for who I was?"

"You've seen enough," he says.

"Will you heal the wounds of those lives, those experiences? Give me their knowledge and whatever they have to teach, so that it stops here."

Under his careful hands, I lie back in the grass as he takes the pain of these experiences out, filling me with light, warm and comforting as the sunlight beaming over his shoulder. Somewhere in the heat from his hands and the rays shining down, I know that I never have to relive those patterns. Now, I can move.

NINE

I want to dive in, go to my Lower World, call the crone to me. It's time to let her in. But the water before my portal is shallow, a giant mud puddle with spittle for a waterfall, thick and lethargic as me. One hand in, and it's not water, but murky slime, a gelatinous film. Grasping, I pull it, ripping a hole large enough to see lively healthy water, fish and new plant life growing within. One light toss, and the muck flies over my shoulder. Dive, and I'm in.

This side of the fall, I hear drum beats echoing through the portal. The rhythm gives the strokes of my swimming cadence, purpose. Coming out of the cave, there is still the steady drumming, voices singing, a great celebration in the Dreamtime.

Hundreds of the tribe are there dancing, blue bodies whirling, blurring against bright orange and yellow flames. A tall man whom I've never seen before comes forward, his hand offered. He leads me through the swaying bodies to the other side of the forest until I hear only crickets, leaves rustling in the breeze. It's black night in the woods, and he leaves me alone.

I'm unsettled being alone here, yet peaceful at the same time. I'm not alone, though. There are others here, near, watching over. An owl hoots high above me, and safe, I can rest, wait for a vision to come. I prop myself against a rock, fold my hands in my lap, and close my eyes in waiting.

Closer by, I hear the owl, a rustle in the trees to my direct right. Startled, I sit up straight. It's not Allusius. It's not *my* owl. I feel him inside me, his expert vision cutting through the darkness, revealing that the owl I hear scuffling near me is the Crone Goddess, the new guide. I can't see her with my eyes; only when I close them do I see her blue aura in the nearby bushes. And although I want her here, need her here to give the answers that no one else has, I'm terrified. I don't know what it is that causes me to fear her.

Slicing through the fear in my mind, I hear her say, *Everyone is afraid of Me.* No one has spoken out loud, but I hear it just the same.

I consider her words, consider then, that I must be as terrified as anyone who would meet her, and in my mind I ask, *If everyone is afraid of You, why are You coming to me?*

There are whole moments of slowly creeping silence until I hear, *Because you are the one that I always come to.*

She's walking around — I hear her — still hidden in the woods, some place intentionally where I can't see her, even if I open my eyes. When I look around, I see myself now and in other lives, with different bodies but always a blue woman and owls, the moon, Earth, and healing. In some lives, we are the same, she and I, one body. In others, she hovers, whispers, always near and watching as she is now.

You're Cailleach, aren't You? I know who You are now...I found You in books. They say You're a Goddess who lived before the Celts, a Goddess of Death. You're the hag born at Samhain. You preside over winter and rest at Beltain.... They say You're a crone until someone is genuinely kind to You, then You become young and beautiful.... You're Arthur's Lady of the Lake.... They say You had many husbands and built the mountains of Ireland.... The people feared You, but they honored You.... Crone.

She doesn't respond. I think I've angered her. I hear no words but glimpse her ashen blue skin behind my eyelids, a shock of white hair, and long black cloak wildly whipping in the wind with her arms raised defiantly on an ocean cliff-side. It's a small victory to me, knowing that she's sending me this vision, affirming that she's Cailleach, *Cailleach Bheara.*

My hunch was right. But how do I rationalize what I've seen of her in journey and read of her historically? How can she be an ancient Celtic Goddess, yet have a connection to the young Native American on the plain and come to me at the same time as part of this darkly complected, timeless South American tribe? Aspects of time and culture blur in her presence.

Confused, I ask, *Who are the people, the tribe?*

They are The People Of The Sun, reborn into many nations.

The First Tribe, I remember. Who we all came from, who we were before the Fall, *reborn into many nations.* That knowledge feels recursive, like something I should've always known but am just now learning. Getting just that tiny bit of information from her, I'm terrified all over again as I know there's much she needs to tell me, and I don't know if I'm ready to own it. I'm not proud of feeling intimidated, and I'd hoped that despite her crone nature, she could be a little comforting about what I've been shown. That hope seems irrational now as I understand more and more her Warrior Goddess nature.

Here with her now, though she's hidden from my sight, I see that comfort has no place in this part of my healing. Right now, I need motion, progress. The things I need help with can't be comforted, only changed. And change is what *she* has come to me for.

This time, I speak aloud. "Why do you continue to come to me when it seems for so many lives, I didn't heed the call? Even now, in this life, I've been stuck."

"Are you questioning my judgment?" She speaks aloud, too, yet remains hidden in the dark.

I reason out a response for what seems like aeons but is probably just a few seconds. Regardless, I have no easy answer to her question. One way or the other, this journey is going to change everything, so with complete honesty I say, "Yeah, actually, I *am* questioning Your judgment."

"*That* is why I come to you."

Involuntarily, my hand claps over my mouth, suppressing nervous laughter and relief. I know my eyes must be huge. I release the breath I didn't know I was holding and prepare to begin knowing what all of this is about now.

"When is the first time that you came to me?"

Stars. Night and stars, mountains, a waterfall...the place I know now is Powerscourt, County Wicklow, Ireland. I remember the fear I had seeing Her in that very place, in the journey with the blue light that lit the hills, then the flocks of stars swooping down as the sky pursued me. I'd begged Simon to get me out. I didn't know it was Powerscourt then. I didn't know it until that same fear returned when in waking, I stood on the rocks of that very fall. But even then, I hadn't known why I was afraid. I still don't know, really. Though I see now, even while she's still hidden in the forest around me, my fear has never been of *her* but of something she knows, something I haven't remembered.

"When else have I met you?"

"Many times."

She's pushing me to focus, and I'm avoiding asking what I really want to know, so I take a breath and reframe.

"In *this* life, when was the first time?"

My back itches, pressed into the rough fabric of a couch, and a tiny thought with a tiny voice says, *a seven-year-old would never put up with this*, burning, *save them all*, and the blue haze hovering in the middle of the room, the mirror, headlights, him, me...*her*.

I press my cheek against the rock, tears sliding down my face and the stone's smooth surface.

"Why are you crying?" she whispers.

I forget. She's a warrior. Comfort is not on the agenda.

"I had no idea it was you who was there. I knew I wasn't alone. Even that night, I felt someone watching over me. But how could I have not recognized you?" I stand up, wiping my face as events and details fall into place. "I always wondered where that thought came from — that a seven-year-old wouldn't *put up* with what he was doing to me. I mean, I was just a kid. What kid thinks things like that? I always wondered where I'd gotten the idea that he *could* be stopped, let alone that I could make that happen."

"But you did."

"Yes, with your help."

"*You* did it. I was merely there."

When I close my eyes now and look into the forest, I don't see Cailleach, blue, or anything. I just see that little girl in Wonder Woman Underoos waving to me, and she's smiling, safe.

The night is quiet, except for the sounds of my crying. Cailleach doesn't try to soothe me or talk, just gives me time to soothe myself, which is as it should be. Who else could possibly comfort this memory but me? I know she's waiting patiently for me to do just that as she has apparently waited for years.

She's the one I've been looking for and at the same time holding at arm's length. If I accept her, I have to accept that she was involved with that part of my life and I'm not happy honoring that connection. I haven't wanted to think that *any* part of my spirituality could be related to my experiences with incest. In fact, it's never crossed my mind that incest played a role in shaping this part of my spirituality, beyond what doesn't kill me must have something to teach me. I've thought all of my life my lessons, from just that fact alone, must be many.

I want to ask how in all her goddessness she could be there that night and not do something, not *stop* it, but she did. She gave me the knowledge that I could stop it myself. Using every evasive kid tactic I could, I made sure that I was never left alone with him again. It was no easy feat, and I remember it all too well. That night was the last.

I want to be angry at her, but all I am is grateful that it stopped when it did, that it didn't get worse, that it *wasn't* worse. It stopped because in the only way my childish mind could comprehend, an ancient death goddess told me that I could be my own hero, that I could stop it by just turning one year older and putting a little ground between that man and me.

She has a power beyond what I've attributed her, far beyond anything I could imagine. She's the shaman in me, the crone, the one who sees spirits and they seek her. I drew on her power when I was a child to get out of a hurtful situation as I must call on her now to move on in my life.

"Thank you, for coming to me and moving me out of that pain," I say, finally having found my voice again. "Thank you for continuing to come to me, for bringing help to get me out of *this*."

"I come because you will it so," she says softly.

"Yes, but you *came* when I needed you then, and you've tried to come back now, but I wouldn't let you. I was afraid. I'm sorry for that."

I begin to cry again, but there's more I have to say, things she may already know. Just the same, I have to hear myself say the words.

"Please know that there's nothing that I have to save myself from anymore and nothing that *you* have to save me from," I whisper. "My life isn't that way anymore, and I've devoted everything I am to healing it. I need your help in a different way now. Please tell me, how can I use the energy you brought that little girl, that you bring me now, to move on and fulfill my life purpose?"

She steps out of the shadows, and she's quite short — three, maybe three-and-a-half feet tall. She wears dark blue robes, every bit the hag.

I step forward to greet her, and she circles me, looking me up and down. From behind, I hear her sniffing the air, lightly prodding at my clothes, using every sense to assess me.

She examines my chakras, my spine purring, warming beneath my muscles where she touches.

"You're in really good shape," she says.

"Took me long enough," I throw over my shoulder at her. I mean to be funny although I am kind of serious, too. It has taken a long time.

"It took as long as it needed."

Her tone is firm, and her point taken. Self-deprecation has no place with this warrior woman or in my life. I'll leave my futility where I stand as it's only counterproductive to the work we do here.

As I wait under her quiet scrutiny, from behind, she walks through my body. The soothing mist of her is a balm. It's a quite different tactic than I'm used to, without doubt a very presumptuous and assertive act on her part to pass through my form without permission. She's testing me as I tested her.

She crosses through in front of me and stands a full height of at least eight feet, a bright blue-white owl, the white owl that the tribeswomen made of me.

"Why the blue?" I ask. It permeates everything related to her.

She says, "That was the color that We preferred."

Simple enough. "Why an owl?"

"Because it's the bird that sees all things. Nothing can be hidden from it."

As she speaks, I'm captivated. She is alluring in her own strange way. She can be calming and horrifying, stern and serene all at the same time. I marvel that she is what I've needed and what I haven't been.

"You cannot fail, Kelley," she says, and I look up at her, recalling that she hears my thoughts. It strikes me that I've never been called by name by a guide before, and she indeed has my undivided attention.

"Then why do I fear failure so much?"

"Step inside. See what I see."

I do, but in her body I see nothing, feel nothing. Maybe I'm not doing this right. My heart chakra flutters with that possibility, so I pay closer attention.

Images come then, me in stiff denim blue skirts over full petticoats. Hands, many hands, busy about my waist, hugging and pulling me into embraces. I'm a pioneer woman of the mythical American frontier, yet she's timeless and of no particular culture. I am in constant contact with the flow of people passing by. Children and adults run up in throngs for hugs, then shuffle on by on their way, satisfied. This woman is maternal but not a mother. To her, they are all her children. This is how Cailleach feels toward every creature.

Apart from this vision, I sense nothing else inside her. Being in her isn't so different from how I feel, though I expected more to this, more awe to wearing the guise of a legendary Goddess. I thought maybe the mysteries of the universe would be revealed, knowing all the questions *and* their answers. Mostly, though, I feel like me. I'm disappointed, though I shouldn't be. She wants me to see something here, and I'm just not seeing it.

And then I notice complete silence—not just muted or muffled, but there is a complete lack of buzz, hum, white noise. No editor is censoring, no self-consciousness, no tension. Such a lack is new to me. Within her, all I perceive is utterly blissfully peaceful quiet. In the quiet, I have a crisper, more vivid perception of everything around me. There is no internal filtering, no analyzing of sights, sounds, or feelings. This peace is freedom, and I let it flow through me.

I'm the pioneer woman again, only this time I feel what the people approaching me for hugs are feeling. Some of them are sick and in pain. Some want more than just a hug, and others are just grateful for the few seconds of attention.

I pull back from the vision and allow myself to become the quiet, understanding its meaning clearly: Cailleach extols the highest intent with every gesture, divining *only* the highest intent of every creature, every soul in the Universe. Inside Her masterful quiet, I feel my connection to all things. I realize that we're all a bit of relaxation away from being gods and goddesses, from being able to see the real goodness in life. I'm sure there's more that distinguishes them from us, her from me. But all I know is my breathing, feeling steady and healthy, firmly rooted inside me, and nothing else matters. That's enough to make a Goddess for me.

She speaks then, and it startles me. I jolt and realize I've missed what she said.

"I'm sorry?"

"Cailleach," she says.

kai lyuuk.

The way she says it is rather different from the pronunciations of the texts I've seen, and I know it's an honor for her to confide this in me.

Now I'm self-conscious, comfortable enough wearing her, but I see the differences between us. I think I've overstayed my welcome. Taking a step forward to part from her body, I'm just that—one step in front of where I stood a second ago. I must look nuts raising my leg higher the second time, goose stepping, but I only move forward again. We are merged still, and she makes no effort to step out of me.

"Is this right? Are we one?" I tremble thinking that she is eager for us to merge. I don't feel ready. I don't feel *worthy*.

"It is," she says in unison with Simon, who now stands behind me. I jump upon hearing his voice.

"You are the manifestation of me, of what I bring," Cailleach says.

It feels strange for them to both be here, and I want to cling to Simon. Instead I just take his hand.

"What happens now?" I ask him, fearing he may go, now that I have accepted her guidance and she and I are walking together, literally.

"You have access to her knowledge, to her message and abilities. In her, you are not just *aware* of the spiritual presence of every creature, you are *in touch* with it."

I nod, but I don't feel too sure. We take a step in unison, and we're back at the celebration in my Lower World.

"I understand things better," I tell him. "No doubt. And I feel differently. My perspective is different. But how does this change my everyday *life*?"

He doesn't respond, and I wonder why he's silent, thinking of the silence I have in Cailleach. I'm not afraid of her now. And I don't feel stuck. Just the *feeling* of her motion is more than I had when I came here. I'm only beginning to understand what she has already brought to my life. I can't imagine what else will unfold with her.

I notice as I'm thinking this, Simon steps away from me. Did he think I wouldn't notice? I know that he must be distant for the time being, but it hurts. I've trusted him with everything, and I can't imagine being without him. Even if the incisiveness of Cailleach is what I need, I still badly want the comfort of Simon.

"I don't want you to go," I tell him. "I don't even *know* her." It sounds silly to say, and I hope I haven't insulted Cailleach, but I don't understand why Simon must step back in order for her to take precedence.

"You *are* her," he says. "I will always be near. I will always be your guide, but you need her guidance now as well."

"Do you have to go for me to have her guidance?"

"You are in more than good hands." Simon smiles, gesturing to Her and the whole tribe, which has gathered around us.

"Why does he have to go?" I ask Cailleach.

"Because his time with you for now is finished."

I know she's right. It's time for a woman leader who doesn't just bring protection, she teaches it. She will push me into my own, and I need that firmness now.

It's right, I hear from my High Self *This transition is right.*

I can't go against it. I open myself to Cailleach, knowing that in spite of everything I've learned of her, acceptance is still a leap of faith.

"Accept this change. Let it work in your life," my High Self advises, now standing on the slope with us.

I honor the words of my High Self. She is the highest part of me, my direct connection to Spirit, and her counsel has never led me astray.

Good things in, good things out, I hear Cailleach say from deep within me. It's good, it's right. It's exciting to have her in my life!

"What are we going to do now, Cailleach?" I whisper to her as we near the portal back to waking.

From within, she says, "Everything."

TEN

I'm above my Upper World, across the rainbow bridge, waiting in the clouds. I've been taken by a messenger, some guy in a crisp brown business suit, to meet my Higher Power and find out why I chose to be mortal again, why my Creator needed me to return. I intend to learn the purpose we decided I would fulfill by living. It's a logical progression for where I am now, it seems. Cailleach walks with me. Simon and Allusius are always near. The tribe always has a book or two for me to gather. And I know bits of what I'm to do here—enough to know I don't know enough. So, today's the day. I'm going to meet God.

A great marble stairway rises out of the clouds and floats on nothing. Humanoid figures wait at its base, standing guard, I guess. Another form is on the bottom step, an animal, though not one I recognize. Just because, I keep my distance, standing a few feet away on a landing.

Maybe I'm doing something wrong or I'm in the wrong place, wrong frame of mind, because my Higher Power isn't here. I hear no trumpets, see no light streaming down, no procession or cherubic choir. I've gone through a lot to be ready to learn my life purpose. Just getting here was a big production—climbing above my Upper World, crossing the Rainbow Bridge, traversing more clouds to keep up with the suit, and God's not even here when I get here. The messenger led me to this place, so it must be right. Pacing, I look for something to happen in God's reception area.

Out of the corner of my eye, I see it's now a dog. The animal on the steps has shifted into a dog. As I watch, it becomes a young Hindu girl dressed in a sari. A gold chain loops her crown, dipping almost to her bindi.

She smiles at me, then becomes an old man of sixty, maybe a bit younger, wearing layers of robes and dusty sandals.

That feeling comes, the one that starts on the back of my neck and crawls up my scalp as I realize that this shifting form is God, and He's been here the whole time I've fretted His coming.

It can't be! But it can...it is. He is really old and rumpled around the edges but sort of glowing and exactly like everything says He is—commanding and serene. Although I never read that He shapeshifts, specifically, or that His ambassadors are men in well-pressed brown suits... and everything I thought I knew... is... wrong. Those old tapes playing in the back of my mind about repentance and falling on my knees, punishment and rewards... To even *think* those things in the presence of this odd changeling standing before me is ludicrous. His hands are folded in supposition at His waist, patiently waiting for me to do something besides stare with my mouth hanging open. I don't feel any pressure to do anything, though. I can just study Him, and it's OK.

This is my God.

I was more afraid to meet Cailleach.

I'm not afraid of Him at all... now that I know who He is.

Watching Him watch me, He has no expression on His face. How do they do that? Allusius, Simon, Cailleach. Their expressions can appear so perfectly still, blank even, yet they project so much. With Him, with God, I feel perfect love, not a lover or a parent, not a teacher or guide. It's all of those and more, at once. He loves me infinitely, and because of that love, I wanted to come back, to live and do something useful with the life He gave me.

I step toward Him, finding my voice. "I've come to learn my life purpose, why you sent me back."

He speaks clearly and without inflection. "You are an example of one who lives with Grace."

Well, that was easy. And I'm flattered. I take a deep breath, pondering His words. I do live with Grace, balance. I like to think that I do in my way, honoring All That I Am, my connection to All That Is, the Universe, God... Keeping myself in balance and healthy... The knowledge of all being well no matter the circumstance. I think that's living in balance. I think.

No sooner have I begun to unravel my own state of existence when He says, "But you don't just live with it. You're willing to die for it, to suffer any consequence of being true to yourself. That is balance."

Because if I don't, I'll die. Don't know where that thought comes from, but it follows His words like a promise, a vow. He stares at me, and I know that there's more to this, so much more than me learning my purpose.

Being 'true to myself' I've never equated with balance or God. They're both such charged concepts, and my beliefs about both have changed so much. I equate being true to myself with survival and healing, not my spirituality. So then why do I hear myself saying, "But they'll kill me!"? Why do I rush to Him and throw my arms around His waist, sobbing? I'm thoroughly embarrassed by my display, not embarrassed enough to stop.

I should be grateful to have my purpose all spelled out, but I'm too frightened to let go of Him to be thankful. All I know is I never want to go back to waking or walk on Earth again. I don't want to leave Him, and I don't know why. I don't care why.

Everything is silent except for my strained sobs. He strokes my hair, and nothing in waking has ever made me feel so safe. Ah, but He was ready for this outburst. He saw me coming because He says calmly, "You are to teach the people how to find their own balance, to be true to *themselves.*"

He can't be serious. Yes, He can be. I've known I'm supposed to work in some healing capacity with people my whole life as some sort of counselor, therapist, and more recently a spiritual teacher. Why am I rejecting that notion now that it's confirmed? Why am I suddenly so afraid of knowing my own purpose? What is it going to require of me? I stand and back away from Him, not feeling very safe anymore. I've had my fill of compassionate protectors with tough love comfort.

Angry, I look Him straight in the eye, and as callous as it feels I say it anyway. "I'm *not* Jesus."

Again, with no inflection, no emotion, He says, "Yes, you are. You all are."

I'm numb hearing this, the implication of His words appearing to me as one of His on a cross, another sitting still and silent under a golden tree, countless others starving in the presence of feasts, burning alive for this state of perfect balance, for the state of knowing their purpose and despite despair, fulfilling it. None of them do these things because their God tells them to or because they won't have a God's love without it. Their passion for their purpose of living in balance is beyond the mere love and devotion to a Deity. It's a devotion to peace and happiness that only manifests by being true to themselves, *each* self, which to God is the ultimate fulfillment of the ultimate purpose.

I should be so dedicated, so at peace in myself that I could fulfill what I told God I would, not just out of duty to Him, but of my own desire. Can I do that? Can I be so true to myself, so graceful that I would risk everything in my life to remain so? I have a hard time believing that if His others knew at the inception of their lives that they were going to be killed for living in balance, that they would have still done it.

"This is why *You* sent me back," I say, "Why did *I* want to come back?"

More visions come. I'm a young boy, maybe fifteen, in a short white toga. I'm lying on a chaise in a sunlit marble room somewhere above Everything, talking with God, jotting notes in a little steno pad. God's different, too. He's younger, maybe thirty, but still dressed the same as He is now. I ease up to the edge of my seat, elbow draped over the arm of the chaise as I speak to Him.

"I want to teach them from my own experience, from knowing life for myself," I hear this boy that I am say. "I know that will mean pain, but I want to experience all of life. I want to reach out to people from a place in common, not in theory."

God leans forward in His seat, His smiling face mere inches from mine, and I hear Him agree.

The others knew they were going to die and so did I, in every one of those other lives as a shaman.

I slump to the cool marble under the weight of this information. How did I get off track? What made me this woman who is afraid to go out from her God and fulfill her chosen purpose?

With the callback comes the answer to my own question, and as the drum beats furiously, I know that I've never been off track. It's all been my own learning, gaining experience, even this search for my purpose. I'm right where I'm supposed to be.

Satisfied with what I came for, I rise from the floor and thank Him as modestly as I know how.

As I begin to descend the Rainbow Bridge, I hear Him call after me, "You don't have to seek new experiences anymore. You are true to yourself. Your experiences are enough to teach others to find their truths."

I nod and thank Him again, turning to hurry over the bridge.

Again he calls, "Kelley?"

"Yes?"

"Happy birthday."

Twenty-nine, today. My birthday has long been framed with complicated symmetry. And as I open my eyes on the place at this moment in my life that I've chosen to be, I think this may be the most complicated.

In the haven of her branches the wind is barely noticeable. I'm gently rocked, gently rocked. If it wasn't for the swollen clouds pressing down and the sheets of rain pummeling the ground beneath, from the heart of my tree, I wouldn't have guessed a storm was upon us.

Now that we've unloaded the car and settled into our rooms, I can finally draw a breath. It's such a relief not to be on the run anymore, even if rest is only for a little while. We're glad for a place to stay, away from everything, although it's in some god-forsaken place that has no foliage, just flat as far as I can see... dust, dry brush... nothing I'm used to.

Except him. He's usually an actor on TV, but he's here in my dream as my lover, and every time I see him, I stop what I'm doing and stand still.

We have Baby. I'm so glad we took her, that we can save her from whatever it is we're saving her from. My little cousin. My little Baby. I just know, every time I look at her I see myself, and I'm glad that I can step in and act on her behalf. She is, after all, just an infant.

He stays busy. I don't know where he is or what he's doing because I don't see him very much. But I know he's busy and he stays busy so we can be well.

There's nothing like the freedom of being on the run with your man and knowing you walk in each other's' souls. And tomorrow's Baby's birthday.

She turns seven.

It's all fuzzy waking up in the dream, and he's not here. I don't know where he is, but I know he's busy for us because we're on the run, walking in each other's' souls.

Today is Baby's birthday.

I walk down the hall and peer into a room where I hear voices. I'm not sure who the woman with Baby is, but they talk and they are talking about sex.

I hear Baby say my lover's name, but I don't believe her.

I peek around the door into the room, and the woman is on the bed with Baby, changing her diaper, and I feel replaced.

They talk like housewives, about keeping their men and fucking. I hear them say fucking, and I hear them laugh seduction.

Something is creeping in on me, and I don't know what it is. It's something familiar like someone I know tapping me on the shoulder, only I never see the face when I turn. I only see Baby, and when I move into the doorway and look into the new diaper, I see hurt scattered like red flowers and a bright red jelly sandwich smeared down her legs, up her belly. I see her, and my body aches from something familiar tapping me but not on the shoulder, and I think it's time to wake up, only I keep looking, step into the room.

And she's bragging about it. Baby sees me standing horrified, and she's bragging. And I hate her because she doesn't seem to realize that she's a baby and that her flower is now a smeared jelly sandwich. Except that she does know and she likes the sticky patterns on her legs.

She thinks it's just fine, but I touch her inside her insides and they're broken, misplaced red goo. I can tell by the patterns that it was he who smeared them, and I think it's time to wake up again as Baby and the woman discuss my lover and his prowess as if I am unaware.

As if she wants to hurt me. As if he is hers.

The Baby child.

That I must protect.

Yet when he enters the room, I light up because we walk in each other's souls and I see something in his eyes that tells me to keep looking in them, that in spite of this, he is whom I have always known him to be, walking in my soul. But I hear him whisper to Baby, "Hi, Sexy," thinking I don't hear. He knows that I know what no one admits, and there's something else in his eyes. But I see the mirror above the chest of drawers and how there is no light reflected. And I remember that today is Baby's birthday, and I am transfixed, and this time I wake up.

ELEVEN

It's cold, autumn, dark in my Middle World. My hair whips in front of my eyes, the force of the wind making it hard for me to stand still. Something has changed here, or perhaps it's me. I'm not sure I'm a good judge of anything right now. Since the dream, I'm wounded all over again. I don't really want to go to the Dreamtime, but where else can I go? Where else can I find out why I would relive my past in a bizarre dream and why it would affect me so badly? And why *now*? I've never dreamed of that part of my life before. I've never had to. I lived it.

A blizzard of leaves swirls around me, then there's only blackness. I can't see the way, but I trace my steps from memory down to the water, dive under the fall, climb into the portal, and out on the other side, it's nighttime.

It's rarely nighttime when I arrive in my Lower World. Simon waits for me.

"Why is it dark?" I ask, hoping he'll quell my panic. "It has to be night sometimes," he replies.

I suppose. Simon's words scare me, so I don't ask any more questions. I don't know when it happened or for how long, but I'm balled up on the ground, shaking, mortified. I don't want to be touched. I don't even like the feel of my own hands clutching my arms to my chest or the ground pressing in under me.

Defeat feels like this, like not wanting to be touched. It feels like filth that soap and water can't clean but contaminates everything I touch. Defeat feels like my private hell has been exposed as if I can be mortified more than I was when my nightmares were my waking.

My past more my present than now, I'm violated *again*.

I should watch what I ask for. I call in this new Crone guide, talk to God, get the ball rolling, and a dream comes full on, in my face like his breath was on my cheek those years ago. No getting away. The dream grips me, but I can't let it go. I see the face of the lover from the dream, and I sense him in waking now, like when I looked into his eyes in the dream. Like if I can just look in them long enough, I'll find in them everything to make this all okay.

But nothing is OK, and I'm wondering how could I put *him* there, someone I don't even know, and feel such love for him and *from* him as I did in the dream? I hated him while I loved him after what he did to Baby.

The waking knows it's not even him who was the monster in my life, knows that the Dreamtime put that man there, and really, I need to know why. I just need to ask.

Simon pulls me into his arms and I'm limp. His touch aches like bruises. He carries me to the medicine circle, sitting before me on the ground, letting a sparkling pink dust fall from his hands onto the top of my head. A hazy pink aura surrounds my whole body. I hold myself, rocking as Simon works, though I feel nothing. He's bathing me. I know he's healing and comforting me because I'm calming somewhere inside. It's just knowledge that I'm calming as I feel yet undone.

Glitter swirls around me, in me, and I'm trying to catch my breath, remembering I'm with Simon, I'm safe, I'm okay, it's okay. I can ask now.

"Why did I have the dream?"

I look up into Simon's face, but he remains focused on the motion of his hands conducting the sparkles through me.

"It was something you needed to see that you didn't see when you were little."

"I don't understand," I say, focusing on staying calm. The dream, that last night on the couch.... I turn it all over as Simon works the pink dust, but nothing's there. Nothing that I haven't seen every day for the last twenty-two years.

Trying to take it deeper, I ask, "Why was my cousin the child in the dream?"

Silence.

"She, Baby, willfully hurt me in the dream. She wanted sex with the man who was my lover, and she intentionally betrayed me after I'd saved her. Does that mean that when I was little and being hurt, I was betraying myself? That part of me wanted it to happen?"

Silence. We've been here before, in the depths of self-sabotage and the many ways it can manifest. Baby was a perfect representative for that.

"That actor, I don't even know him. Why was he there? Of *all* people, why was he one to hurt me in the dream? He wanted it that way with Baby, yet there was something that he wasn't saying. There was *more*."

Simon doesn't reply, and I'm shaking, frustrated with understanding that it's not time for me to know these things. Other knowing is pushing to come first, and I'm afraid of what that is.

I mull over various scenarios for what I need to see about my life, that the dream chose to show me such strange characters and context. But the more I think about it, I'm humiliated that *anyone* was part of the dream, even though they aren't actually in my daily waking life. 'Concerned' doesn't even cover the potential spiritual attachments that the dream could have created between my painful experience and the people in the dream.

"Simon, did any part of the dream affect the people who were in it?"

Guilt creeps over me as if *I'm* an offender, as if my dream made *them* dirty, just by virtue of them having been in it.

"No," Simon says, "though there is a cord between you and the man from the dream, a spiritual significance."

I don't want to know that. "That's not what I asked."

"Isn't it?"

I don't respond because I don't know what I want to know. I only want not to feel mortified anymore, for any reason, *ever*. Such is the kind of humiliation that for the majority of my childhood kept me from myself.

Simon works with his brow crumpled in concentration, still drizzling pink sparkles over my head. I'm able to talk and interact with him now, so I know he's clearing out something. All I feel is lonely. More than lonely, I'm connected to nothing. If I didn't I trust Simon, I couldn't be here at all. I don't think I could face anyone else right now.

"The dream, I need to know the meaning. I'm sad, humiliated like the abuse just happened, *again*, and I can't live this way. I need to know if there's something more that I need to address. I need to know if I've left something undone about the abuse. Please tell me."

Simon sits quietly, and I wait for his reply nervously tracing circles in the sand beneath us. Eventually he shakes his head and says, "You want to do so many things."

I'm full at his words, chest tight, throat choking, blocked with big expectations and too little time. I'm overwhelmed with urgency, panic, and I can't breathe. I grasp my throat, knocking pink out of his hand. I flail, grabbing at Simon, but he keeps working as if nothing is unusual, as if I'm breathing fine.

Seeing that he's not coming to my assistance and that I'm managing to stay alive through Simon's ministrations, I choke out, "I only want to do what I need to." Heal. Love. Write. Work. Learn. Teach. All in a day.

Rest. The idea comes from somewhere inside me. Pretend life is really long. Live it luxuriously as if I've got all the time I need to do everything in this one lifetime. No rush. Do whatever I want. Forget about a life purpose. Freedom from obligation to myself or anything else. Just *see* how that feels. Gulp it down my windpipe. Force it into my lungs.

Try to process it. Make it my mantra. *Rest.* Only, that's not me. Time has nothing to do with my life. There's no such thing as 'time' in accomplishments. There is only complete spiritual, willful application of self.

Finally, I deduce, "I want to do it all." It's loud, clashing with the serenity of Simon, and it sounds stupid, self-righteous even. Who am I to think that I could fulfill everything that I seek in one fell swoop, in one lifetime?

Simon smiles, and I don't know what's behind the smile. Maybe he knew that I want to do everything already. Yes, he knows; I'm the one who can't swallow it. I think it's okay to be that industrious, and I find in Simon's smile the possibility: me being me, turning over every stone, talking with each one. Because that *is* exactly what I would do.

He stands, then walks into the woods. I follow Simon to a clearing where a stone precipice rises from the ground. I recognize the Goddess Garden in my Upper World. We must have taken a shortcut.

The garden is considerably more detailed than the last time I was here. The familiar four stone steps lead up to a landing with an eight to ten foot drop past its edge. The rising is topped by a great arch, and I'm drawn to stand beneath it and look out over the garden. I approach the steps seeing foxes, horses, raccoons, birds, and many other creatures about the surrounding woods and courtyard, waiting, standing in attendance, but for whom I don't know.

From under the arch, I survey the garden, animals and plants all staring intently back at me. It's spring. Flowers bloom, the sun shines brightly above the canopy of green, stray rays glint on new grass. It's the perfect place for an egg hunt, but I don't fit in at all. I'm sorrowful and disheveled in a place of pristine joy. Self-conscious under the gaze of the woodland creatures, I look down at the stone floor, then close my eyes, crying.

A noise brings me back, and looking forward, off the precipice stands my God, only this time, She's a Goddess, absolutely radiant in full white gowns with a pink sparkling tinge. She's a woman, but I know it's Him. I recognize Him by His love, a warmth I never want to be away from. She stands flat on the ground, but towers above me and the arch. I have to crane to see Her face.

I'm speechless, but I want to talk to Her, want Her to hold me. Mostly I want to run because She has come unsummoned into my world and that means whatever is happening to me is big, bigger than me, abuse, or a dream.

She's so beautiful! Her guise is late twenties, early thirties, with thick dark hair, light skin, light eyes. It's hard to be frightened, feeling *how* beautiful She is. And it's strange to see Her as a woman, though it doesn't really matter how She appears to me. It's *that* She's here that matters. Still, that She is female is somehow extremely comforting.

Just standing here with Her, I know that She loves me. I felt love from this God-being when It appeared to me as a male, but it's even stronger now. It's not sexual, not romantic, not parental, not platonic, but somehow all of those. In Her presence is all the love I've felt for anything and everything in my life, all at once. *This* is the only way to describe my love for my Goddess.

Her arms surround me cradling, kissing, holding me for a long time. While in Her arms, I have smatterings of feelings, impressions melding my life and the dream — his hands groping my little body on the couch, the joy of having saved Baby to be betrayed by her and the lover who was in my soul, my birthday, waiting for the light in the mirror to save me. It all comes, but with Her I don't panic, just feel it, feel *through* it, moving through the anxiety, to the calm I feel in Her arms.

There's something else in all of this. Don't know what, something about the dream and that night. Having these feelings come, yet not panicking. It's as if spiritual connections are attaching these things, and my brain can't process how. Her calm is how I can know.

I can let this come together, held by Her. I could completely forget the dream, the man in it, my history, all of it to just stay with Her and always feel this peace. I'd never leave Her side again. I'd never try to figure any of it out because it wouldn't matter anymore. I never wanted to leave Her, even before when She appeared to me as male. I clung to Him then as I cling to Her now, afraid of what the world has in store for me.

As soon as this fear emerges, She opens Herself to me, raising Her arms high above Her head, robes parting to reveal glowing white light in Her middle. I rush inside, greedy for Her comfort.

Within Her is a great white circus tent, and I walk around in it exploring from one end to the other. I hear voices, muffled from the outside, their shadows moving on the fabric of Her interior. She's with me, but I'm alone.

Maybe it's the creatures that I saw in the courtyard scurrying, getting into wardrobe, pushing props into place, shuffling together a set to reveal insightful knowledge in a beautifully choreographed parable, clearing everything up. I listen to movement all around the tent, thinking someone will come get me, dim the lights, then project some great wisdom off the white screen of my Goddess. In lotus position, I get comfortable on Her hardwood floor.

I wait, but nothing happens.

Life is going on *outside*, and I begin to feel as though I'm missing it. There's laughter, the smell of food cooking, voices busily engaging in lively conversation. Excitement wells up in and around me, like waking up to the joy of a holiday. Only there's no waking. I'm just here, inside Her. I'm not part of life, only aware of the impressions of it. Hiding inside Her, life takes place without me.

I want to be part of it. I want to see what's going on. Throwing open the heavy canvas flap, I step out into the village across the crest of the mountains in my Lower World. It's a medieval time. Everyone is dressed in dark gray or black colors, no one standing out from any other. But as soon as I register how dismal everything is, from the bustling bazaar a woman emerges dressed in a pink overdress and dark crimson underskirts, the same crimson piping on her sleeves and neckline.

I should know her, but I don't. Maybe she's a mother, a past of me, an aspect of me, my Goddess... I don't know.

Whoever she is, she takes me in her arms and I'm safe again, secure, shielded, and for a few minutes, I weep against her shoulder. She strokes my hair, smooths it from my face, murmuring comfort. For a few moments, I relax, and I'm at peace with relaxing. Everything is quiet, calm, still.

Still! I'm not moving. My life is upside down, and I'm wasting my experience here by crying to this woman. I don't want to leave the safety of her, but no matter how long I sit with her or anyone, I'll never truly feel comforted. I can't be comforted. Comfort won't resolve why I'm here. Wiping my face, I pull away from her and run. She follows and tries to pull me back, but I stumble back into the busy footpath of the village.

Instantly, I'm not in the village anymore, but sitting, again, in a white space. It's not a tent; rather, I'm in a solid room, with no shadows or voices, no delicious smells and laughter seeping in from elsewhere. Inside, there's only me, cut off from everything. No Higher Power, no High Self, no guides. I try to feel them, but there's nothing. Something will happen in a minute. Someone will come. There'll be a noise, a vision. *Knowing will find me.*

But it doesn't. Nothing finds me, nothing happens. I must be missing something. There's only silence, stillness, complete deprivation within, without. It's not the sweet peaceful silence I found inside Cailleach. No, this is painful. This silence follows loss, the primal silence before the scream. My pulse stretches my veins to force blood through as my breath pushes my lungs to expand and contract. Waiting, there is nothing but me and waiting, and there's not going to be anything else. No one else is going to make something happen for me. I have to let go. I have to surrender everything, what I know, what I don't know, what I want to know.

Where you are going, you can bring nothing with you. I remember Simon's words, realizing more and more what he meant. Focus, bring the breathing down, heartbeat under control, release the expectations. Be silent. Settle into nothingness.

For a split second, everything is black and I'm dead. I am not in a body, and I know this feeling. I remember it.

Then I am reborn as myself into this life. I cry every night. Everything hurts, every touch, every look, every word, and I withdraw. In my dreams are hands on my throat choking the life out of me. In my waking are hands on me still, touching and burning during the day. At night are specters, shadows from the corner of my eye pulling my hair as I wait for sleep. I'm home alone after school, terrified. The dull thud of a plastic flower keychain hitting the metal doorframe as it unlocks is salvation. The creak of the door closing follows a body coming in, but I'm lonely. I feel nothing. I am nothing but paralyzing pain, from the cradle until now.

I want to hide, go somewhere to lie still, still and alone. I know that's bad. All this motion in my life, and now I want stillness. I came all the way back to this life only to spend it pining to get back to my Goddess. I don't know what to do, where to go, who to... Cailleach. She'll know what to do. She was there that night. She showed me the way out. She can tell me about the dream and show me the way through this.

"Cailleach, please come." My body feels sucked from the white space, and She's with me in a forest. Even though She's here, I say it over and over, "Please come to me," deriving comfort just from the words themselves, relief at just having *thought* to summon Her. I know She's here, but I don't see Her, just feel Her presence and confidence, and it's enough.

"Remind me of our discussion from our first journey," I ask my Goddess, who stands by Cailleach.

She replies without pause, "You're here to love yourself, to teach them love and life. To awaken them."

Slightly different wording than before, but I remember it: Find my own balance, my truth, and teach others to find their own. Ah, yes, I remember now: Inspire in others to accomplish what I can't fulfill in myself. I have the nerve to ask Her to remind me of this, having known lethargic sleep and awakening, and now the frustration of beginning to begin somehow back where I started.

Still, I try to rationalize the way I feel about events in my life *knowing* what my life purpose is. "I do love myself," I tell Cailleach. "And I love everything like it's my whole life. I give all of myself over to what I love. That's what loving is, to me."

My words sound futile. Exactly who am I trying to convince as I stand here afraid to leave the side of my Goddess, essentially giving myself over to nothing? If I can't give myself over to Her, to unconditionally trusting the course we chose for me, to leave Her side and come back to waking to fulfill it. How can I unconditionally love anyone, anything else in my life, even myself?

"Kelley, I *am* your whole life," my Goddess says. "That's what a God is. The summation of All of *you*. Everything you can feel and experience and love in life is Me. That is why I am with you, *always*."

I'm comforted, and She didn't even touch me. No hugs, no caresses...just the few words. Instead of fretting, I just needed to remember to carry Her comfort with me. That's all it took.

Now, I can proceed.

"What about the dream?" I ask my Goddess. "Why were those other faces in the roles that I know were really me and my abuser?"

"It was going to happen no matter what role you played. You would have been affected the same," She says it matter-of-factly, yet as passionately as when She says, "I love you."

I sense myself falling into total devastation, then rebuilding, that same scene playing over and over with different roles. Some spirit son of mine abducted, castrated, murdered. My own rape as a child, domestic rape as a wife, my daughter beaten, raped, and left for dead. The theme of sexual assault was going to be in my life, one way or another.

"*Why*? Why did it need to happen at all?"

I'm dizzy now, and I'm choking, *again*. I'm a baby and my father leans over my crib, shadows surround him. From behind the bars, I wonder what he wants. That speculation and fear clouds my thoughts as he picks me up, and we go to the kitchen to make pancakes. Yes, I see that even then when unwarranted, fear of sex and men was not new. I brought it into this life with me.

Mom is here now. I'm a young teen, and she knows what happened to me. I told her everything, and she asks what I want to do about it. I want to paint my toenails, but I don't tell her that. How do I know what I want to do? I just yell at her to get out of my room, then I don't see her for days, maybe weeks.

When I do see her, there's little left in her to see. Watching us interact in the silence of our lives that followed, it's apparent that the effects of one man over a handful of years change all our lives forever.

My sister. We are in a diner in the mountains, and I'm eighteen, telling her for the first time. She takes my hand and tells me she knew something had happened, she just didn't know what or when. When I look at her, I see that I never want to know life, any life without her, although my words part us, instilling in her the need to look into her own past.

My extended family, except for my abuser, stands around me, huddled, but they're distant. I've told them as well, and they don't really want to be near me. They don't want to believe or feel anything. They all back away until I stand alone, again.

I'm completely separated from everyone and everything I've known in this life, silent and still. But this time, it's perfect. Everything is gone in that stillness, and I'm me *without* pain, me *before* pain. And although I'm elated to be totally free from that hurt, I'm infuriated that this is the first time I've ever known this kind of peace, that my life had to implode first.

"Abuse or not, *why* does *anything* in my life need to happen?" I scream at Her, and I don't even care that She's Spirit. I don't care who She is, what the reasons are for anything, and She lets me yell at Her, though She doesn't respond.

I know the question is redundant. Nothing *needs* to happen. Need is choice come to fruition. Still, I flank Her wanting to know more. "Why *that* face? Why was he the lover of my dream?"

"The dream was not just yours, and the role he played in it has no bearing. You felt safe enough to let it be him, to work the issue out with *him*," She replies.

I'm not choking now. I just don't remember how to breathe. Do I breathe in dreams? I don't remember. I've never noticed. I only remember that every time that man walked into the room, I had no breath. I lost the ability. I knew him, exchanged something with him. It was a two-way street. Not sure what or why; don't have to know. I'm just honored, thankful that his presence woke me enough to move me to this moment.

I know the next logical question, but I don't want to ask it. I want the answer without having to say the words, but my mouth goes before my brain and it's out. I can't stop it. "Why was *he* my abuser in this life?"

Immediately, She follows, "A great debt was owed between you."

As much as I wanted it, I don't think I really expected an answer. Survivors are supposed to ask why just to be healthy in the concession of asking, not to actually learn the reason. I always knew there was a reason, which is *why* I never really asked. On questions asked, the Universe has delivered, bringing me both an answer and a debt. But did I owe him? Did he owe me?

There is a tug in my chest as I grapple with making my mouth move. "What was the debt?

"He owed you. He gave his life for you."

Obviously, I heard Her wrong. Gave? Raping me is giving his life for me?

He gave his life for you, he gave his life for you....

Like a savior? Maybe I don't know what a savior is. Maybe I don't have to know what She means. Maybe I don't have to clarify it. I can leave it ambiguous, like my feelings for him.

But how did he give his life for me? Did I say that out loud? Did I say it all because I don't think I did, yet She says, "To be consumed with guilt so that you can grow — to wake you."

Don't want this to be intuitive, but it already is, without thought or processing. Clear. Knowledge. I *know* his soul. And I loved him. The soul who paid this debt is the man who abused me as a child. He is that soul, and although it's entirely impossible for my brain to grasp, I know him and his actions beyond the context of this life. I know what She says is true.

The protocol of anger and forgiveness, the cliché of blood and water doesn't even apply here. I've felt an agreement between us for years, a willing participation with this man who is my family, though I never could bring myself to conceive of what that agreement was. I thought learning it would undo me, undo my healing, and nothing was worth that risk. But I can't carry the terms of this agreement one step farther.

Wherever you are, I'm standing before you. Hear me.

"You no longer owe me your life. Your life is yours to do with as you wish. You don't have to feel guilt anymore. There is no more debt between us. We're equal. We are balanced." I close my eyes, and I feel Her with me as I repeat it, releasing the debt, releasing myself.

As I speak, I sense someone's here, joined us. If I turn to my left, I'll see it, a pale blue mist that will be him. I look over to find a young man in his late teens, maybe early twenties. He has a very small frame, but he's not fragile. He's dressed in a light blue tunic, has short blond hair.

Just seeing him is loving him, missing him. I recognize him immediately, though he looks nothing like the one who hurt me in this life. I can't deny though, that the love I feel for this boy is the same love I felt for my abuser as a child before he hurt me, and even for a time after. I try to distinguish them, separate my feelings for the soul from those for the man, and I can't do it. Here and now, all I remember is loving him, trusting, and nothing after.

I'm not dazed or jaded. It *happened*. It's not that the hurt didn't happen, but looking at this boy, I feel the context under which it happened, and all there is is love. I realize that if I can feel love for this man on any level, I can love anyone in my life. If I could have the opportunity to see the love, the spiritual essence of everyone in my life as I see him right now, I would always be able to find something to love in everything, even the things I don't want to.

As I stand with him, he's sorrowful. He isn't crying, but there's great distress in his face. He knows the history that played out between us since we last met in the Dreamtime. He knows there was a great deal of pain inflicted on me from the culmination of our agreement. I'm sad for him as I sense his regret at being the cause of that pain.

Taking his hands, I say again, "You have no debt to me. You no longer have to carry guilt. Your sacrifices have culminated in my awakening, and our agreement is fulfilled. I love you. *Thank you*."

Though he doesn't speak, I know he loves me. He doesn't have to say it. I feel it, know it, and that's enough. And he accepts my words. He releases the debt, and it's time for him to go. There is no more reason for him to stay. We hug for a long time, and I'm truly sad that I won't see him this way again for a very long time. He leaves and already I miss him. But I can let him go, let *this* go, peacefully.

Immediately, I'm back at the arch, my Goddess waiting. "Thank you," I tell Her. I know it's anti-climactic, but there's nothing else for me to say. It all feels done, and instead of making a dramatic departure, I begin to make my way back to my Lower World.

Simon waits for me patiently to return with him to the valley. With exhausted steps and renewed spirit, I head toward his outstretched arms. About half way there, I realize that for the first time, I'm willfully walking away from my Goddess. I don't feel torn away or obligated to abandon serenity with Her to become part of the mundane. I'm moving on, beyond, *with* Her. I stop, teetering like a toddler between doting parents, looking at my guide, then back at Her. She smiles proudly, silently telling me She's always with me, always speaking to me. As long as I remember Her voice, there's no more loneliness, no more constraints or conditions for me, just love, *balance*.

I continue into Simon's arms and tell him, "You are my good friend." It's an odd thing to say after all we've been through, but somehow it's the most important thing I can say to him right now. He smiles, pride beaming from him, and we go arm-in-arm through my portal.

In my Middle World again, it's fall, dark and cold. I walk away from the portal feeling as if something is missing, like it's not time to go yet. I linger but see nothing, feel nothing. Slowly, curiously, I make my way back to waking. Wind blows high in the very tips of the trees, rolling in, down, to gently stir the foliage at my feet. I stop, watching autumn ripple past me as it pushes my hair from my eyes. As I stand in the breeze, I hear Her say, "I am with you. I'm here." And I know from this moment on, when I hear the wind whisper high in the trees, I'm not alone. My Goddess is speaking, passing through to me.

TWELVE

I'm pacing as Simon draws, charcoal colors on textured paper. Kind of like the good ol' days, when I would lean on a cloud and ramble until he indirectly helped me figure things out. So far, we're on par because there's no reaction from him as I rant.

"I *know* the bigger picture has reasons I don't see. I'm *trying* to see them, I really am. There's just still something missing. There's still something making me feel, bad, incomplete, or I wouldn't be losing my mind now. Would I?"

The question is directed explicitly at Simon, but he doesn't acknowledge it. Just keeps drawing, so I keep talking. Maybe that's all I need to do... talk.

That's it! He's not adding commentary so that I can just talk. I can just say all the things I'm feeling and then how I feel will make sense.

"I understand the things I've learned from the dream." I talk through it like I'm working a geometric proof, a mental list of things that when logically put together create something greater than themselves. "I know the lessons that are before me, and I'm at peace with having chosen them: I want to learn to love better, *higher...*" Yet the proof doesn't work or I've put all the pieces together incorrectly, because I'm still frustrated. "I'm struggling, even after everything I've learned. Loving the man who hurt me, in spite of what he did."

I cough, choking on the words as they catch in my throat. With my hand over my mouth and shaking my head, I continue. "How is that possible? To love him *and* have gone through everything I have to be well? Healing that has been *hard*. It's been painful. Loving him now makes me a traitor to all of that, everything I've been through, even though I know that's not true. It *feels* that

110

way, though. My soul is going one way while my brain is going another, and I don't know how to help them both be at peace."

I pause, satisfied that I've thoroughly laid out everything. Simon smudges colors with the heel of his hand, and for the first time that I ever recall in our visits, his colors blend. Violet and yellow create a vibrant red.

"I understand that he made a huge sacrifice for me. I know he did, and even though I haven't actually seen him in years, I have no doubt that he's suffered tremendous guilt in this life for what he did to me. He did give his life, in that sense. And I know everything that I've sacrificed to be standing right here—things like sanity, intimacy, a billion life experiences I was afraid to have, and tons of other pieces of myself I sloughed off along the way. I just feel like if I don't resolve this split in my feelings and honestly learn to love him *as I live and breathe in waking*, not just in the Dreamtime, I won't be able to have that spiritual love for anything else, ever."

Nothing, not even a blink from him, as with perfectly clean hands, Simon picks out another color.

"What do I have to do here?" I ask, moving in closer. "Talk to me like I'm four. How am I supposed to resolve all this?"

"Learn to love them all." He says it like it's no big deal.

"That's what I'm trying to do."

Patience is gone. I glower at Simon as he smooths his hand across the page. His one broad stroke of bright red screams *Compassionate love, not just acceptance, tolerance, indifference!* I stare at the wise charcoal, stilled by the word "indifference."

Simon turns to me and says, "In Spirit, there is no such thing as indifference."

I sit down hard in a chair that before I began sitting wasn't here. I know I can't force feelings that aren't there, can't dismiss ones that are. And I can't pretend I don't love, can't hate what I haven't loved. I'm so close to getting this. Something is trying to come together.

God is the summation of All of you, everything you can feel and experience and love in life.

It sounded so easy when She said it. But why am I remembering that now?

I shake my head, cradling it in my hands, trying once again to put it all together. I've thought that I was stuck all this time in learning my life purpose, carrying it out, healing and keeping my body well. But I wasn't stuck. The red charcoal says I'm intentionally avoiding my feelings about any of this. Indifference. So now that I'm feeling, it's a big rush of things all at once that *seem* to conflict.

Conflict can't coexist with indifference because indifference doesn't feel enough to conflict. I've been trying to force myself to feel indifference toward my abuser and my family when I've never felt indifferent at all. I love them, even though I haven't always wanted to. If I stifle one feeling, I stifle them all. Can't pick and choose. And love can't be polite "we've got company" love. It has to be messy, passionate love—the way I love Her—that depth, for everything, *especially* things I don't want to love. I must have compassion for him. If I discard one feeling or one person, if I discard him, it will take away from every other feeling, every other relationship in my life forever.

I've worked myself into quite a frenzy reasoning all of this out. I understand, but the split between my thoughts and my feelings is still there. Propping my chin on my palms, I ask Simon, "Am I a failure if I can't do this?"

"There is no such thing as failure, only readiness," he replies.

His words carefully remind me that what I don't accomplish now, I will later or in another life. Indeed, in life there is no failure, only infinite opportunity to become ready. Even just the talk of failure wastes my precious energy in arriving.

"Is not being ready holding me back from doing other things, from doing things I really want and *need* to do?"

Silence. Simon's silence always confirms me.

Even asking the question allows me not to take risks or be responsible for my own success.

Stop acting like you didn't choose this place in your life and find the way to move beyond it, my High Self says. And she's right. What I've been doing isn't working, and I've exhausted my inner resources for healing. It's time to do something else.

Finally, turning from the easel, our eyes lock and Simon says, "Go see the shaman."

THIRTEEN

It's been three days since Simon told me to come to the shaman. I'm here only minutes when she says that she has chills, that my guides are close. Her guides, however, tell her I need to do more before she can help me. The avoidance must be lifted first, and more healing is needed.

I quickly come through my portal where all of my guides await me in my Lower World. My High Self inspects my chakras, clears them. When she and my guides have given me a thorough once-over, I sense that I am running.

I recognize it as a place I've been before. Cold burns my lungs as I run over a ridge. They're chasing me—men, armed and angry. I fall at the crest of the ridge; I can't move. Their leader stands above me, sword drawn. The soldier runs me through, pinning me to the ground through the breastbone, between the shoulder blades. My vertebrae throb in pain even as I lie among the soft pillows in the journey room.

I *have* been here. I've died here before for being what I was, what I am now: a woman seer fleeing an army of men.

I'm falling back though I'm lying down, back to the moment in my past at which I can heal all of this. Dizzy, I'm floating outside myself, completely weightless, and my head is swimming. A baby screams at the beginning of another life, one that I've glimpsed before.

I see a kitchen in a dark medieval stone structure. I'm here, somewhere watching or interacting, I don't know which. All I know is a man rapes a woman bent over the dining table, hurts her.

Which am I? Him? Her? Frantic tears sting my face as I try to figure out which. I quiet my anxiety, trying to see the lesson. I need to know who I am. Maybe I'm the man? My sexual assault in this life would be penance for committing the same in a past life. Or maybe I'm the woman, another in a string of my legacy?

Only I'm neither. My gaze settles on a child, her child, their child, seven, maybe eight years old. A girl hidden behind pantry shelves in the corner is me, and they don't know I'm there, don't see me. They don't hear my mantra, *I'm never going to do that. That will never be me. I am not sex is not me.*

I find myself chanting along with her, glimpse the shaman scribble on her paper as the girl whispers. "No, I'm never going to do that, never be me. *Rape is sex is rape,* and I'm neither of those." I'm nothing but a child hidden, far, far away until her little hands are bound, mouth gagged, hurt, one in a line of many lives that are mine.

This pattern is nothing new to me, though I'm panting in exasperation. Coming back to my intention, I ask, "Simon, how does revisiting this past help me to heal the avoidance I've created now in moving forward?"

"Because what happened to that child *did* happen to you in this life, and it's not what you thought it was. It is *more* than you thought it was."

"What was it?"

The scenery changes. I'm in a TV-lit room, and many presences are with me. I don't feel like me, and my abuser doesn't feel like the man I know him as. Rather, he is his young soul in light blue, and my highest spiritual aspects are all present. I sense no pain or fear, only a great awakening. Even under his hurtful hands, the human child aspect of me loves him, in spite of his hands, and I hated that part most. Hating and loving, all at once. That's where this split between my feelings and my mind originates. But feeling our spiritual presences on this night, I feel only a very high love. My questions are moot.

"Is this the time that I can release the hurt of that child from the past life? How does it relate to my current issue of avoidance and indifference?"

My golden High Self holds a silver platter in her hands. On it, I stack the killing times and the assaults of every life to let her take them from me. The platter's contents tower above her head. Pride radiates from her smiling eyes, her arms never bowing under the weight.

It's time for her to go now, take it all away, but I can't let go. My hands clasp hers, pulling her back. She gives me a loving supportive look, though I feel ashamed for not being able to let go. Finally, I release her and she walks, getting smaller in the distance, but never arriving. I'm still holding onto her.

I'm missing something. I've left something undone or I would be able to let her take these things I no longer need to carry. "What is the exact wording of the vow that little girl made in that kitchen?"

That I would never forget. *Rape is sex is rape.* It's all bad. All sex is rape to her.

That I would never allow. *I am not sex is not me.* And she won't be part of sex, under *any* circumstances.

Although I don't believe those exact thoughts, I can feel where they have manifest in how I live, how I love. They have rooted into my life.

"What is the replacement belief, to take the place of those, to allow me to heal the issues now?"

I hear no words but feel the warmth of Simon's love, his presence. I listen closer, but still hear no words.

Then, slowly it comes, an image of me tied in a cold stone cellar, bloodied and hoping someone will come for me, yet terrified when I hear footsteps. Unable to hold myself up, I'm propped in front of an entire community. I hear weeping as attendants stoke the flames that are waiting for me. They lead me toward the fire, saying words about me, calling me names that mean bad things to them, but mean shaman to me. Just before I'm thrust into the fire, items of my practice are forced into my already torn womb—crystals, an herb pouch, and a torn scroll.

I don't see myself consumed by the flames. Instead, when my moment of death comes, I see the rape of this life, a couch, a TV, and a mirror awakening me, bringing me back to Spirit.

I see that my experiences with sexual assault are about more than feeling love where I don't want to. They are about the cause of disruption of my balance being the thing that has brought me back to it.

The living room of this life was no stone cellar, no dark kitchen.

How do I accept this?

How can my spirituality be connected to rape in any life?

I can't move, I can't do anything but sit with the emptiness of feeling that nothing I have is my own. Everything I have is just a result of something that came before.

Can't something just be mine and have nothing to do with the rape?

Can't I have something without what he did staining it?

My relationships, my habits, sex, sense of well-being, even my birthday I'm used to reclaiming these from rape, but Spirit, too?

I can't stay with this, can't stay here. Doesn't matter what I lost, what I never had. I can't avoid this, can't hold onto it anymore.

"How do I resolve the irony of this contradiction?" "There is no irony. What silenced you was the only thing powerful enough to wake you."

Simon's love confirms, and his truth burns. My abuse and spiritual path are not and have never been separable or distinct. I didn't realize that until now.

"This circle has come full," Simon whispers. "All you needed was to see it."

"Yes." Maybe I say it, maybe I just mouth it, I'm not sure. I know he's right.

Smaller she becomes, my High Self, walking away until she and the silver platter disappear completely into the West, the setting sun, returning to fill the empty spaces from what was taken out with her light.

"It doesn't have to be that way anymore," she says.

"Good!" I say, throwing my hands up. She laughs at me, and I can't help but laugh with her. This is good. We have done well here although I know it's not finished.

"What insight do you have on learning to love my family in this higher way?"

My High Self quickly replies, "You already love them."

"Yes, I do love them." She's right. The problem has never been that I don't love them. I just have needed to allow myself to *feel* it. Squeezing out that last bit of indifference, I give her another stacked platter to take away.

"Is anything about all these experiences still embedded in me that will get in the way of healing from this point on?" I ask my High Self.

"We have finished with it."

"What do I do now?"

My High Self only looks at me, and I hear Cailleach say, "Let the shaman look."

FOURTEEN

The shaman tells me she is at a high place in her Upper World, at the level of creativity and spiritual will, where creativity yields a creation.

She flies upward, carried back to the beginning of life, at a cliff dwelling in smoothed red rock in the West. She sails off the edge of the cliff, saying it's the ridge where I was chased by the army. Only this time, I'm not killed — I keep running and fly off of it, beyond.

"This flight represents healing the gap you feel between your soul and brain, your avoidance," the shaman says. "It is now joined in the work you've done today."

Heat flows through me as I sit by the shaman in her journey, every pore of my body opening and releasing.

"The heat you feel is that healing." I'm a bit self-conscious that she senses the heat from me, but before I can comment on that, she says, "Tell me what you need to know now."

"What do I need to do to carry out my life purpose?" I ask her. "I know its subject, its end result, and that I'm to write, but that's all. Define *how* I carry it out."

Her guides move her away from the present and forward to a river that's white with a tinge of gold and pink. The shaman says pink is love. To me, it's my Goddess and gold is my High Self. Moving her still, her guides place her at my birth point with a female presence that is Cailleach.

"Cailleach holds a book filled with light," she says, her words coming in punctuated bursts. "As soon as it is in front of my face, it becomes dark as charcoal. I think I'm not seeing it properly. When I look closer, it's dark only because there's a hand going across it writing, furiously. Volumes of charcoal handwriting, turning the pages black from the many words. Cailleach says that you must go back to the beginning of time, and you will know what it is that you are supposed to write."

"What does she mean for me to go back to beginning of time?" I ask, leaning in.

She breathes deeply, releasing the breath slowly. After a few seconds, she begins to speak quickly again. "You are to go back to the beginning of all your lives on this planet and write pictures of how all these incidents can be interpreted in the light of love. Write about the love that is actually there even though it may not feel loving or the experiences may not on the surface seem to warrant it. That is what your guide says."

She pauses again, then adds, "You need to see the thread of all your lives from the beginning of time, clear to now. See the thread of that... And the number fourteen is very important," she says. "Fourteen stories of the same book."

I don't know what the number means, but when I close my eyes, there are books in green leather binding, each connected. When I open one of the books, its pages are golden light. They're not bound, but are conjoined like paper dolls holding hands, fitted together such that each one shares a connection to every other. All of the books have this same page structure.

Colors come to the shaman, green, deep royal blue, and red. Fourteen she associates with the green, lush Irish green. I look at her then, thinking of the green of my Lower World and the paper doll books, and she continues.

"Blue is royalty, holding true to yourself. Red is love, passion. Do these mean anything to you?"

I nod, baffled by her analogies. Remembering that her eyes are closed, I blurt out, "Yes. I know what those mean." *Home*, the green that is indeed Cailleach's home in Ireland. *Balance*, the blue of Cailleach and the tribe. *Passion*, the red of the love inherent in everything.

Heat rises in waves off my body. It feels like my hair moves in an unseen breeze. My skin burns as if I'm in sunlight, as fear seeps from my pores, leaves for good.

For the first time since the dream, I'm happy, relieved knowing something good will come of all of this. I will create something good not just from the abuse, but everything that has come after it. I don't even have to think or map out a way to make it come to fruition. In fact, I'm so calm, it's as if this creation had *already happened*, and I'm sitting on the other side of it, looking back.

My mind and soul sit together, peacefully. Peace is being able to have any feeling that may come, alone or in combination with any other, and not being thrown off track.

The setting sun of the West, the direction of the death realm, and the heat from my body escort away fear. I don't have to avoid anything, any feelings, anymore. My High Self takes it all away on a silver platter. No longer needed, no longer mine. As the shaman returns from her journey, I lie back in the pillows, relaxed.

FIFTEEN

Back. I've come back with love to see the beginning of my beginning on this planet. I don't know where this beginning is, so instead of going through a portal, I just close my eyes, and ask my guides to lead me where I need to go.

Cailleach takes both my hands, and I find us walking into a sunrise, the opening of the day. Once behind it we stand in empty bright space. The light is the most brilliant I've ever seen, seeing my first sunrise from the sun's perspective.

We go to the exact spot where I entered my first life on this planet, and it's Powerscourt, long ago. The area is more densely forested than when I saw it in this life, the fall and its mountains seeming to rise higher above the valley. There is no more beautiful place than this.

"What is the lesson that I was to learn through all my lives?" I ask Cailleach.

She holds a deck of cards that have hand-painted runes on them forming words, phrases, whole sentences breaking apart and rejoining. Watching them, I know that their constant movement means that for every eye that can read, a different meaning emerges. For every ear that can hear, a unique message speaks.

Cailleach looks up from the card spread and says, "There is so much more than one thing in all things. You can discard no one feeling and the truth of an experience be revealed." Embrace it all. It's a very simple concept when she says it. Though I know that had she said those words months ago, before the dream and the experience of my pasts, I wouldn't have understood. I've loved that which I have hated. Knowing that fact, I realize I hate nothing and can see the love in all things if I choose to. Embrace it all. Have compassion.

"What about the experience of abuse, about *that* night, about the fulfillment of my purpose needing to have a different focus at this time in my life?"

A future aspect of me comes, Fifty-four, and she emphasizes new life. "Allow every experience to bring new life to you. Don't just settle on the pain or joy of an experience, but allow yourself to see all of those things at once, inseparably entwined, yet distinguishable. Every experience holds infinite wisdom and information, if you will allow yourself to see it."

She's me, yet she speaks like my guides. Twenty-five more years, and I get to be her. I must be doing something right!

Without a pause, Cailleach picks up where Fifty-four leaves off. "Until this point in your life, you have understood your purpose to come here and look at these things, but you were limiting what you were willing to see from them," she says. "The focus now needs to be life in everything, and feeling that life, itself, is synonymous with love."

Basic things that have been in my life—bouquets of flowers, graduation, marriage, divorce, death—things that touch everyone's life in some way, all have the love of Spirit. As ordinary as they are, they have some aspect of Divinity. And I make a choice to see it in mundane experiences, a *purpose* in living it, no matter how horrifically it may be hidden.

"But how do I live it?" I ask. "How do I tell others that this love is even possible when it may be wrapped up in pain? It has been very painful for me. What I am supposed to write that can explain the coexistence of love in pain?"

This simple question plunges me into panic. I'm pushed back into the dream and to that night all at once.

I see ink trail across pages from my own hand, yet I can't read what I've written. The message is about my life, yet not the experience of living as I've perceived it up until this point. I perceive the experience of my life through the knowledge of Spirit. I see all aspects of life with eyes of love. I see it as it really was, not just the bleakness I chose to see in it.

Comfortable with that understanding, yet dubious of undertaking such a project, I ask, "Is there anything else that I need to know about this beginning of time spot to prepare me for the writing?"

Cailleach steps forward, whispering. She's speaking, but I don't hear what she's saying. I just feel calmness and sense that I must learn more about her and understand my relationship to her, this goddess, this experience of myself whom she has repeatedly said is me.

"Who are you to me?" I ask.

"You are me," she replies. I squirm, unsettled by the equation.

"What about you makes me so afraid of being you?" I ask.

The many forms of her come then—high angel, saint, blue hag with her owl familiar, crone with the blue aura, the Dark Goddess of the tribe, and many, many owls. In the presence of all these forms of her, I reply to my own question, "It's your power, isn't it? I'm afraid of your power. Such a foreign thing to me because feminine power is what I feel I've never had."

Cailleach stands then with her arms open, waiting for me to allow her in, to want her, to fully call her in. But I can't do it. I'm uncomfortable identifying with this creature on any level. I know it's the right thing to do. I know all the work up to this point and the completion of anything after it relies on my ability to accept Cailleach into my life. Why can't I?

"Help me feel your power from your perspective, Cailleach. Show me how it feels to be you, *to you.*"

I step into her and wait tentatively to feel something, to feel *different.* I release my compulsion to force something to be there, release my fear that there is something there, and just relax into letting whatever needs to, to come.

Breathing deeply and steadily, my third eye opens. With my seeing eyes closed, I observe a golden outline in the trees, the plants. The glow is similar to the way Allusius sees but far more vivid. There's more accompanying what I see. I *feel* associations to the forms that I see. The longer I watch them, the clearer they become. I sense them more strongly.

Souls. Cailleach sees souls as a golden spiritual essence in *all* things: people, animals, stones, plants. Because she sees that life force in everything, she sees only love in all things. The fur, the bark, the actions, the words coming out of a mouth... She perceives them, but they are an afterthought to the joyful spirit inhabiting them. Until now, I haven't wanted to find love in everything. I've wanted some things to be very much unlovable, so I could put them away and have that as a reason not to deal with them anymore. Putting them away is not having compassion for them...

We face each other as I face my fear of Cailleach, of knowing she's been here, patiently waiting for me to remember who she is and to accept her. An invisible boundary that I drew between us more than a year ago now erased, I bring her in, along with a way of love I honestly haven't wanted to know until I could see it her way. This way of love *is* Cailleach: the embodiment of loving the dark unlovable, my thread from hurt to healing, abuse to Spirit. Finally, I understand why I did not want her as my guide. In understanding, I want no other guide more.

Understanding doesn't change the fact that she's a goddess, and I'm human. It's easy to remember things here, but I still have daily life to return to, where it's not so simple. "Cailleach, how can I hold onto your perspective, see the souls and love in all things?"

"Remember that what I see is what you see," she advises.

I sit inside Cailleach, content to stay, and infinitely thankful that she stuck with me all this time and to my High Self for appealing to my intuition to allow Cailleach in. From within Cailleach, I peer out at the valley, see the golden halo in the grasses, in every individual blade, the leaves in the trees, the animals hidden in the forest, the clouds.... I've glimpsed souls all of my life, but that ability became more vivid, more intense when I met Allusius. With Cailleach, they are *perfectly* clear. I see them and I'm not afraid of seeing them or the circumstances in their lives. I'm not emotionally thrown off center. I see them with discernment and insight into their many facets, and how the souls interact with their physical bodies, with each other. In Cailleach, I see souls without losing sight of myself. The best part, though, is they see me. They look to me, acknowledge me, then resume their wafting dance.

I smile, then hear the shifting beads of a rattle around me as Cailleach hovers near. The simple gesture makes our merging complete. We are one, but I find myself falling back, dizzy and unsteady.

"Can this guide, this *Goddess*, be me?" I ask Simon. I need reassurance from him. Despite how good it feels to be with Her, I need his confidence.

"She already is," he, Allusius, and the tribe say in unison. I wasn't aware that they were all with us; now that I see them, I feel their support...and my own.

Carefully culling, I pour through my belief system for anything that would interfere with merging with

Cailleach, searching for anything that would block my ability to believe that I can be with this goddess. Sure enough, I find what I seek... an attitude, screeching with an angry female voice, *You're just a girl. You're just a raped girl, and no matter what goddess you put on, that's all you will ever be.*

I know that voice. It's the voice that right before victory tells me I can't win, tells me I can't succeed at anything. Even though I know what it says isn't true, the voice is still there, somewhere, playing over and over behind everything I want to overcome into my life. It leaves me feeling that I can't be anything, can't be who I am on any level. I know now, that if I can't be who I am, I'm not experiencing balance. If I'm not living my truth, I can't accomplish the things I need to.

Quickly my High Self responds to this attitude, removing the voice, filling its void with the words, *I am who I am.* She brings that knowledge through my entire being, making a permanent change in how I think about myself, my daily habits that reinforce who I am to myself, how I treat myself. She heals it all. As my High Self works, there's no longer an impediment inside me; there's only Cailleach and me, standing together.

"What else do I need to address at this time?" I want to make sure this is all done, complete.

Somewhere on the periphery of our gathering, I sense anticipation as if they were waiting for me to ask this final question. With a sudden rush of energy, I hear, "Welcome!" as my guides and the tribe inform me that I have stepped across the boundary of myself and am now standing among them, an informant in my own spiritual council.

Cailleach steps forward from the group. I see her as a separate creature, yet I feel us still merged. I can see her, interact with Her outside me as I do Simon or Allusius, yet we are the same being. Cailleach extends her hand. I take it in mine. When I withdraw my hand, it's heavy, warm. Turning it over, I find a large oval sapphire embedded in my left palm.

"To help you remember to look for the love in all things," she says.

"Thank you." I marvel over its beauty and weight in my hand as she steps back into the fold.

Golden light comes down from above me, wrapping and filling me as my High Self takes the healing we've done in this journey through my physical and etheric bodies. The light comes over me, through me, down deep into the earth beneath my feet. It anchors me there, exuding out into my life force, until I am who I am. The love that I see in the things around me, I have in me. My feet rooted, I kneel and taste the earth—the rich grit of centuries of mountains, seas, trees, and returned bodies ground fine—to this connection on my tongue.

SIXTEEN

As I climb the spiral stairs to my Upper World, I consider what's before me now: I have to go back and see it, see it *all*.

"I've decided to surrender my experiences," I tell my guides. "I'm coming to the Dreamtime to see this life with love. Instead of looking at it with my eyes, I'll close them, so I can truly see." I say this and close my eyes tightly, asking them to lead me. "Give me the experience of this life with the knowledge and love of Spirit, and I'll honor *whatever* comes." I focus on the intention, saying it over and over in my mind.

I squint, open one eye, then slowly the other. It's dark, but I recognize that I'm in Powerscourt. I see my Lower World fully for the first time. The valley where I've always come, with its pond, stream, and mountains, I just couldn't see the land completely until now. Before this journey, parts of it were lost in my periphery, hazy and not filled out. Before, the edges faded into nothingness when I tried to pan over its far reaches.

When I look for its boundaries now, there are none. The landscape rolls beyond where my eyes can see. The forest to my left spans far and wide, sloping down to the pond and its trickling stream, the dryad tree perched just above. To my right are the sand medicine circle and the forest beyond it. But instead of just sloping down to a blur of the stream and woods, I see the fall of Powerscourt, mounds of rock worn smooth, washed in the spray at its base. The mountain supporting the fall towers above the valley of my Lower World and the village that I know lies on its other side. The mountains rising beyond this one are connected by a worn trail, looping and spiraling between and over valleys and crests as far as I can see.

Finally, I have the ability to see all of my Lower World, and I can travel anywhere in it.

A loud tapping, rapping, echoes through the valley, distracting me from the landscape. I hear the tapping even above the break of the fall waters.

There at its rock base, an old woman strikes a huge flat rock jutting from the ground. She holds a smaller rock high above her head in both hands, then slams it into the earthbound stone. Over and over, she holds the stone up, then claps them together. It's a strange ritual that I don't understand.

Quietly, I approach her. Just as I grow close, she flies away, vanishes into the night. Intuitively, I take up her stone, cold and heavy, then bring it down hard. The loud clap of the rocks together resonates in me as I feel the root stone and the earth beneath it absorb the vibration I send. Dark night echoes the raps of stones in the distance, and I look up to see hundreds of the tribe lining the mountain top above the fall. They're dressed in heavy furs and pelts as if for winter, but each of their hands is bared. In them, they hold small stones that they clap together, sending a vibration back to me. I don't know what it means exactly, but they're not only responding to my summons, but summoning me as well.

I blink, and it's a spring day, quite sunny and warm. Children run across the valley in pastel play clothes and shiny Sunday shoes. They seem to be seven, maybe eight years old, running free, laughing and playing hide-and-seek and hopscotch, skipping rocks on the water.

I play, too.

One girl, a blond in a floral dress stands apart, and I recognize her as my mother in this life. We play together just like the other children, but there is a spiritual recognition between us.

For hours, our little group runs. Then spent, lying on our backs in the warm grass, we try to catch our breaths, laughing all the while.

As we lie on the slope of my Lower World, something calls, something above the fall. I'm drawn to it but hesitate. The children, however, have no fear, and instead of taking the footpath up the mountain, they head up the craggy slope of the fall. I follow, climbing the rocks from base to top, staring at the water the whole way up, listening, or seeing — which it is, I'm not sure. We just know something is there, calling us.

The whole time we climb, we play. It becomes a game, to make it to the top and look out over everything, to go to the beginning, where the fall starts. In no time, we stand at the source of the fall, splashing, tasting the water, our toes numb in the cold flow as we look over the edge of the world.

No sooner do we arrive at the top, than down they go, this time scaling the rock down the right side of the fall until I can't see them anymore. One-by-one, they are disappearing behind the fall. Again I hesitate, thinking that I'm not safe climbing a waterfall like this, all the while trying to keep up with them. I feel okay, though my brain cautions as I follow them behind the water.

A cave is here, shallow with just enough room for four of us to sit. They've found something in the center of the cave floor. No, they haven't found it. They've come to retrieve it. They knew it was here. One of them picks it up, and they each take turns holding it. I can't see the object, only their faces, which are lit with awe.

Carefully, purposefully, the blond girl passes it to me, her eyes full of knowing. I look into her eyes, waiting for her to speak, but she doesn't.

Looking down, I see the cool smooth gemstone that she's placed in my hands. It's heavy, bigger than my whole hand, and it has a mottled bright blue, dark blue and black coloration—lapis lazuli. I smile as this gem bears the colors of Cailleach.

I hold the cool lapis, marveling at its smooth polished finish. Its top is round like a head, then sloping shoulders elongate into four three-dimensional sides, converging in a blunted tip. I glance back to the children who now wear wraps as the tribe did when they stood on the ridge earlier. They beam with pride. Curious about its purpose, I look back to the gemstone and to the children again, only they're gone. I'm alone in the cave.

Carefully, I climb back down, with only one hand to use this time as the other holds tightly to the lapis. Slowly, I make my way down and back to the valley.

"What do I do with this?" I ask Simon, who defers me to Cailleach.

She takes it, handles it deftly, with familiarity. Facing me, She places it into my heart chakra, and it connects with my mind, body feelings, and soul, warmth spreading throughout. The gemstone speaks to me, saying that as the sapphire Cailleach placed in my palm reminds and enables me to see the love in all things if I choose to, this lapis lazuli in my heart connects me to the love in all things. It makes me an active participant spiritually, giving love, receiving love. It is love's conduit in me.

With the gem in place, for the first time, I sense that the Dreamtime is alive unto itself. I span over the Lower World I see in my Dreaming, seeing that this place isn't just a backdrop providing a stage and setting for my personal growth. The Dreamtime is an entity that loves me, serves up exactly what I need. When I'm tired, it supports me with lands to stand on, a sun to light and warm me when nothing in waking can. It bore a moon to whisper to me who I am. This place comes to me as much as I come to it, and as with my Goddess, I can breathe it, be it, take it with me everywhere. I'm never apart from the Dreamtime. With this gem in my heart, I am part of the Divine. I am the Dreamtime.

Another spirit comes, the Spirit of the North, revealing herself as the direction of the body, of Earth. She's dressed in blue and white with bits of frost on her skin, in her hair, and in her wraps. She's beautiful. Kneeling, the North draws a circle around me, starting in the East and moving West through each direction, the sun's path. From the East, she begins another circle on top of that one, this time moving East, the closing of a day. In her drawing, she presents the birth of something, and its transition into something else, full circle.

Blowing through cupped hands into my heart chakra and the lapis, the warmth of breath from the North Spirit stirs inside me. There is heat in my ribs, and as I look down, my chin almost resting on my chest, I see dim, then vibrant light, catching, spreading blue fire through my body. Beyond my body it shoots out of my crown into the sky, out of the bottoms of my feet deep into the Earth, not just warmth but illuminating blue heat. This is not light coming into me; this light is pouring out.

In the glow, everything becomes clear. The things that I've seen, that I've wanted and been looking for, finally I feel their completion. The books, the lives in them, the healing, the outcome. I don't just see the closure of these things, their product and payoff, I feel their completion, my purpose fulfilled. The anxiety that I've had about knowing what to do is gone. I've already set in motion what is needed to make this all come. And with this feeling of completion comes the security of knowing my actions and my process have been right.

The North leaves, and Cailleach comes. She rattles around my crown, East to West, then once around my feet in the same direction. It is done. The energy of the lapis is sealed to me, available to my life. Cailleach whispers warm on my cheek something I don't hear, but I calm from Her speaking just the same as I accept the completion She has given. I realize now that in order to go back and see my life with the perspective of love, I needed Her to bring this peace first.

I descend the stairs as the blue and white owl, then fly back into my chest, into the beautiful starlit room of my center. Even though I've left my Upper World, I sense that I take everything with me everywhere I go in all of my worlds. I look back over my shoulder to see my Lower World melding into a long cloak attached at my shoulders, billowing out behind me in a long train that swirls into the portal behind me as I leave. When I open my eyes and sit up, I'm still that owl. My heart purrs with the light of this crystal, and I know the Dreamtime has sent its star to keep me company. I'm ready to see the events of my life with love.

SEVENTEEN

I leave my direction and instruction to my guides. They will take me where I need to go to see my life. I'm drawn to Powerscourt, my Lower World. It's night, and Cailleach is here. She wears many layers of wraps, a bright blue cowl under a dark wool cloak, the same as mine. She's older than I've seen her recently, her hair coarse and white, but not quite that of the Crone. I'm a younger, dark-haired version of her.

She smiles at me, knowing what I've come to see. I feel her pride in me. "Let's walk to the moon," she says. Happily obliging, I take her hand.

We walk beyond the stream to a distant mountaintop where the moon's belly rests just above the ground. So close to it, I sense that the moon is alive, taking part in our journey, not just hovering above it. We sit in the moon's wake, the breeze lightly stirring our wraps.

Cailleach prepares a small fire, then kneels before me. She slits her left palm, then presses bright blue blood to my third eye, over my cheeks and chin, the four corners.

"Remember I'm with you," she says. "We all are. You're safe."

I know that I'm safe, but I take her words very seriously, readying myself I don't know what to expect coming back to this. I'm not naive in my travels anymore. I know that in the Dreamtime, sometimes things are unsettling. Love won't eclipse the painful feelings I had in hard times, but it will temper them if I let it. Love will give me the ability to see what I couldn't see before. I'm afraid to undertake this, of that there is no doubt. But I'm more afraid not to.

Cailleach leaves, and I breathe my expectations into the fire, deep steady breaths, watching them go up in cinders rising from the flames. I sit back on my heels facing the fire, warming my hands, moon beams all around me.

Slowly, I drift back to that night in the car, just me and Mom on the way to his house. Panic creeps in. Not just my panic of seeing, but the panic of my child self. Yanked back to the mountaintop, my eyes fly open and the moon leans close over my shoulder. I wasn't prepared to feel the child's feelings as well as my own.

I know this time, and this time I can see more than fear and panic. I can do this. Holding my hands out to the fire, I warm them, letting the vision come again. And when the heat from the flames has warmed all the way up to my shoulders, I'm in the car again.

Easing through the back door into the kitchen, I see the pizza on the countertop and us seated at the table. He's eating, but she's picking at the food, this very small me seated between the table and counter, while he sits at the head of the table.

I come to kneel at his side, but he doesn't see me. I speak, try to engage him. There's no reaction, no acknowledgement that he hears me. She does, though. She sees that I'm frustrated with not being able to communicate with him. She's upset that I am frustrated, and her concern only embarrasses me because she's a child. The worries of her life far surpass my anxiety of not being able to get his attention. Ultimately, I just want her to know that I'm there for her, so I forego interaction with him and move to her side of the table, kneeling by her chair.

The child looks down at me, afraid and fully aware that she's been left alone with him again. In her face, I see full knowing of what being alone with him means. I also see determination in her face. Somehow it's her resolve that comforts me, *adult* me. She looks back at her pizza, nibbles at it, but I cry. I'm impotent to save her. Even though I've come back to this moment, it's not to help her or change its outcome, but to observe this moment *wholly*. My only power here is in keen observation of the *full* experience, not just the hurt of it. I'm incredibly saddened knowing what I'll see, what she'll feel, and that all I can do is sit back and watch. This experience will change everything, including my perspective on the hurt, but I'm still not happy about seeing it. With this knowledge, I move away to let this happen, back behind the counter, leaning on my elbows. Looking across the kitchen I see that Cailleach is standing between the little TV and dining table.

The dishes are cleared, and up on tip toes, little me drops a fork in the sink. He picks her up, and she's grateful, her arms going around his neck.

I don't understand.

I follow as he carries her into the living room and switches on the TV there.

I don't even like being in the room. I want to make this be different than what it was. I know they are settling onto the couch. I know it will be a long night before she sees the headlights in the mirror. I know with only these things in mind, I'm not seeing what I came here to see. I'm letting my sadness cloud my view.

Cailleach, what do I do? I ask silently, pleading not for a different outcome, but the peace to see it *all* through this last time.

I don't see Cailleach in the room anymore, and I hear no reply. Instead, a tiny hand grips mine, pulling me along. I look around to see that I'm no longer in the living room, but standing on the Rainbow Bridge, heading to the bright light of Spirit. The light ahead of us is so bright that I have to shield my eyes to make out the very small me holding my hand. She walks happily, smiling up at me. We walk, but as of yet, we don't arrive, and I'm confused.

I panic, thinking I must have missed something when I find myself back on the mountain with the waiting moon, fire, and Cailleach. Her hands are loosely folded in front of Her. The moon casts a misty blue glow around Her as the TV had in the kitchen, and I understand.

"I already knew, didn't I? I don't *have* to journey back to that night to see the love. I saw it then when I was little. She saw it and let it happen exactly as it needed to. She did what she was supposed to, what she *could* do." I don't know how I can be so calm about this, but I feel the intuition of that knowledge rooting in me. My relief suspends before me in the night mist as I speak. "I've lived out my whole life with that knowledge, exactly as I meant to. I've just spent all this time trying to remember what I already knew."

Cailleach nods, then puts Her hand over the glowing lapis in my heart. "I've given you nothing you didn't already have. You only needed to remember."

"What about the dream? Do I need to go back to it as well?"

"Yes."

She leans in to me and begins whispering. I don't understand what she's telling me, and I feel nothing but the warmth of her breath on my cheek.

"I don't know what you're saying," I whisper to her. "I'm telling you that it's okay to remember now, to *know*."

I nod, accepting any comfort she will give.

"What do I need to do now?"

I hear Her whisper plainly, "Talk to him."

"Will You come with me?"

"I am always with you."

As she says the words, she fades from my sight. I close my eyes, and when I reopen them, the eyes of the man from my dream are what I see. I'm back in the bedroom where the dream ended, standing at the foot of the bed, look¬ing right at him while he looks back at me.

He's anxious. He leans casually on the chest of drawers, hands in his pockets, shoulders framed well in the mirror behind him. But when I look into his eyes, I see that he's tense. He's been waiting.

"You knew the dream was really about me and not just the baby, didn't you?" I ask.

"Yes," he replies, nodding. His hands fall to his sides, but he still props against the chest of drawers, fingers strumming the outer seam of his jeans. He's sad, a bit detached, yet I can tell he's relieved that I've come back to the dream. He seems to have unfinished business here as much as I do and that surprises me. One day I'll learn that nothing is a one-way street in the Dreamtime. Everything in a dream or a journey is having its own experience with me, not making an experience *for* me. Subtle, yet significant distinction.

As I mull over what I want to say to him, he says, "I would never hurt you."

The words take me aback. I'd never considered that *he* would intend to harm me, despite that my fear of him in the dream was real, and that after the dream, in waking I was leveled. I never, for a second, thought this man meant me harm. He was just a cosmic proxy for someone else from my past. I realize this concern is the cause for his anxiety, and I wish I could have come back here sooner to tell him that I understand.

"I know that." I nod, and moving forward, I hug him. Our embrace is brief but closing just that bit of space, I feel his sadness even more. I step back, realizing how selfish I've been, seeing only how this dream affected me, not remembering that the Dreaming affects everyone in it, and truly, affects All That Is. I had no idea I would come here to calm *him*.

"I'm sorry." He breathes in sharply, throws his hands before him as if he's going to say more, then drops them back to his sides, sighing.

Shaking my head, I say, "There's no need to be sorry. You didn't do anything wrong. I needed to know. I needed a push to go back and see that experience differently, and I'm honored that you came to the dream to help show me."

He nods, squints at me, and cocks his head. "It's all over now?"

"Yeah. It is."

It's strange to say that, that there could be an end to this part of my path. It's stranger still to be talking with him so casually, like I know him, better yet, like he knows me, when in waking we don't know each other at all.

"Can I ask you something?"

He nods only once, but his expression brightens and his shoulders square up.

"How did you come to be in my dream? It's so unlikely that you were.... How did you know?"

"I don't know, really." He shrugs and shakes his head. "I felt the tap on the shoulder, and I knew I had to do it."

"But you *didn't* have to."

"Yes, I did." He speaks firmly but smiles. "I needed this as much as you."

I don't know what that means, exactly. Actually, I don't know what it means at all. I don't have to know because he knows, and whatever it is, it's making him smile. The sadness lifts a bit, and that's enough for me.

"Thank you."

"Thank *you*," he replies, standing.

Silence. Our silence is awkward human silence, not the knowing soulful kind. There is something unfinished here. After a few seconds, I say, "It seems like there's something I need to say, but I don't know what it is."

"You don't have to say anything," he whispers.

This time I'm the one shrugging, and I pace on the far side of the bed, rubbing my temples. There is something more I'm to do here, I just don't know what. "I'm supposed to come back here, to the dream, to see how it would've been had I known the love all along."

"But you did know all along." He follows my pacing, hands in his pockets. I don't know how he can know this about me since I just learned it myself, but he's confident about it, and he's right.

"Yes," I whirl around facing him, and he freezes in place, blushing madly. "But I didn't begin remembering until the dream, and everything after. I didn't put it all together. And I wouldn't have thought to if you hadn't stood out in the dream. I wouldn't have known there was more to look for."

He purses his lips and gazes at the floor, then his eyes snap back to mine. "And now you have put it all together."

I stammer a few seconds, then say only, "Yes." In a word, I know that's it. That's all I need to know from coming back to the dream: I have put it all together.

"Thank you," I say to him again, taking his hand. We hug again, and this time, his sadness is completely gone. All I feel is the quiet stillness that I found in him in the dream, and somehow knowing that I do know him. He does know me.

"You don't know how important this has been to me," he says. He doesn't smile. In fact, he's very somber as he speaks. I don't know why he says it. Truly, I don't.

"No, I don't know. But I trust you. I believe you." We both smile, and the silence that falls isn't awkward. It's... peaceful.

As he turns to go, he takes my right hand in his. Squeezing it gently, a cold dampness spreads through my hand, then he makes his way into Spirit's light. When I look in my palm, I see that he's left a blue and white spotted lily embedded there.

I watch him walk away, his figure growing smaller in the distance. Just before the light completely takes him, he looks back and waves, a flash of blue in his palm.

I open my eyes and sit by the fire, studying the lily, processing all that's happened. Cailleach sits across the fire from me, quietly, patiently warming Herself while I ponder.

"Where do I go from here?"

Kneeling beside me, She whispers, then blows something that I don't see from Her hands into my face. Taking my left palm, She presses it flat against my right, and I feel their centers warming, sapphire touching lily. She raises my flatted palms to my third eye. Holding them there for a few moments, She separates them, raises them open to the moonlight.

Lifting Her palms to the moon as well, She says, "These hands are love. Who you touch is loved. You hold their hands to take them to healing, to the other side of life and death. You are a hand-holder, an angel of death, love, and life."

I understand then my purpose and the influence this Goddess has on me. More than seeing the souls of all things and allowing me to connect to them, She has a finesse in dealing with things that on the surface seem horrible. Yet She knows how to soothe them, call out their beauty. And She does it because She wants to, not just because She has the knowledge of how to.

Apparently, through Her, so do I.

We take our time, hiking carefully back across the mountain, up the slope to the portal, and out of my Lower World. As I leave my Middle World, crawling out of the pond, a parade of animals follow, hundreds of guides, and the tribe all follow me, shaking off water. We are a fantastic spectacle, and we walk back with every step knowing everything is as it should have been, as it is, to this very moment where I'm standing, writing, loving.

EPILOGUE

THE MOON'S MESSAGE

The moon is my mother, sister, lover. I have come to the sacred land of my people to hear her, to mate her into my soul. It is my time, and I have made myself ready.

I wait solitary but not alone.

I will not sleep.

I will not eat.

I will ride the owl's wings into her heart and the sound of the river deep into her belly. I will sit quietly until she has whispered to me that which she has for me to know.

Her words blow softly through breeze and beam. "You are a moon child. Your energy draws from me. Your power and inspiration draw from me. You operate as the light in darkness. You will help me light the darkness of the daylight, of the sunlight. This is my message to you. This is who you are."

Her words give me life. I will remember this night for all eternity. I will live in the light of her, and I will die without the darkness of fear. For when I am born again, she will remind me of this night, of who I am, and I will walk in the path of her light, always.

Greeting the Dreamtime

I was visited by souls of the dead as far back as when I slept in a crib. As I grew older, the dead gave me their death experiences, and lingered for me to help them move on. Not understanding their need, I pulled the covers over my head, terrified, and waited for the sun to come up. Apart from visits with the dead, I was also fully aware of sending away soul aspects of myself and bringing them back at a very young age. I often saw the souls of the living apart from their bodies, which was most disconcerting. I thought if I could see the soul of a living person, that must mean they're near death. Sometimes those living souls did die around the time that I saw them. Most of the time they didn't. My belief system just didn't allow me to understand the nature of souls, their ability to travel from the body and return, or the capacity of a departed soul to reach out to one of the living. I didn't know how significant those youthful experiences were, that there were names for them, or that other people had them, as well.

When I learned of shamanism at the age of seventeen, I began independently studying various cultures of shamanic technique and following an animistic path. I harassed my guides a great deal. At twenty-six I had a strong need for soul work in my own life and healing, and began working with a shaman. Shortly into that work, I realized my spirit teachers were leading me to work with others. In 2000, I established *Soul Intent Arts*.

I am a North Carolina native, though my intuitive path and practice is one of intertribal shamanism, with many cultural, ancestral, and personal influences. Blessing these dear predecessors, my path of shamanism is original and claims no culture other than the one of my creation. Though I describe my personal path as 'celestial shamanism,' I do not seek to teach a branded path of shamanism, but to present the map for you to create your own. My practice may be Earth-based but it is Star-centric. Along with the beautiful earthly devas and elemental allies, I work with a Light Choir of higher beings to co-create connecting with Multiversal forces, and the True Self. I honor life from all of the stars and feel a keen connection to a bigger stellar home, having worked extensively with issues that arise for clients who identify as not being from Earth. I have worked quite a bit with starbeing children, who often are labeled as ADD/ADHD, and with adults who have experienced interactions with life forms and histories spanning other planets and dimensions. To that end, my studies continue and I am engaged in learning various ways to raise and hold awareness on our planet.

I am an incest survivor, so much of my shamanic healing and practice stems from working with traumatic pasts, releasing the karmic patterns of trauma, and manifesting Dreaming into Being. I do a great deal of work with survivors of sexual assault, and am continuously working with my guides to find better ways of bringing light to the community of survivor healing. In my experience as a survivor and co-creator of my Life, and in working with other survivors for years, I've learned that the Dream can be Life, moreover, it already is. Allow it. Know it.

Working with the suffering spirits of land that has hosted recurrent trauma has been a focus of my Druidic practice. It is a blessing to experience All Things through the practice of supporting Nature.

I have worked extensively with women experiencing concerns around fertility, miscarriage and pregnancy, facilitating communication with the spirits coming into this realm, and healing in the mother's etheric field.

I also focus a great deal of work and studies in finding ways to honor the path of those I call *The Tribe of the Modern Mystic*. These are people who, like myself, have had intuitive experiences since childhood but were unsupported (and often demonized) in their path to manifest their gifts. I'm here to create a new tribe of support for children and adults whose lives are blessed with an uncontainable inner knowing.

My shamanic work is quite diverse, and my clients are all over the world, from many cultures. Private sessions help them restore their power with soul retrieval, extraction, and chakra and etheric field balancing. I teach classes in-person and through Distance Mystery School.

All of that said, I am a healer only of myself. Of Life, I'm an enthusiastic student. Of the souls around me, I'm an observer, and good listener. Talk to me about what's going on in your life, and I will help you find a way for you to make your life better.

Be open to the Dreaming.

Dream well,

Be well.

— skh

an intertribal shamanic practice
for Multiversal wellbeing
www.soulintentarts.com

Follow Kelley at:
https://www.facebook.com/s.kelleyharrell
@skelleyh

Follow *Soul Intent Arts* at:
https://www.facebook.com/soulintentarts
@soulintentarts

Read Kelley's open dialogue with souls at *Intentional
Insights – Q&A From Within*
www.intentionalinsights.com

Find information on Kelley's other books and
publications at www.kelleyharrell.com.

CPSIA information can be obtained
at www.ICGtesting.com
Printed in the USA
FSOW01n1948171217
42536FS